Ronald Vaughan

W9-DJE-627

HOLD THEM VERY CLOSE, THEN LET THEM GO

HOLD THEM VERY CLOSE, THEN LET THEM GO

HOW TO BE AN *AUTHENTIC* PARENT

Richard C. Robertiello, M. D.

The Dial Press
New York
1975

Library of Congress Cataloging in Publication Data
Robertiello, Richard C
  Hold them very close, then let them go.

  Includes index.
  1. Children—Management. 2. Infants—Care and
hygiene. I. Title.
HQ769.R5775   649'.1   75–26606
ISBN 0–8037–5376–4

"The Spock Children" is based on material first published
in *The Village Voice*. Copyright © 1974 The Village Voice,
Inc. Also published in *Art and Science of Psychotherapy*.

Manufactured in the United States of America

First printing

To Robbi—
A "good enough mother" to Abra, Eric
and Susan, but most of all—to me

CONTENTS

HOLD THEM
VERY
CLOSE,
THEN
LET THEM GO

THE "SPOCK" CHILDREN:
THE REASON BEHIND THIS BOOK

A particular group of young people, especially young men in their late teens and twenties, have begun to make their appearance in the offices of psychotherapists. For purposes of convenience I am labeling them the "Spock" children. I want to emphasize the quotation marks around "Spock." I certainly am not trying to make Dr. Spock responsible personally for some of the problems I am delineating. Similarly I am not attempting to cast aspersions upon his excellent book, *Baby and Child Care.* I am using his name as a symbol rather than a specific reality. It is a symbol for the prevailing attitudes in the psychotherapeutic community in the late forties and early fifties. I readily admit that at that time I had exactly those attitudes, gave similar counsel to my patients, and in some ways brought up my own children with these ideas as a guide.

These "Spock" children were brought up in liberal, intellectual, psychologically sophisticated homes at about the time when Dr. Spock's book on child-rearing was beginning to have an enormous impact on attitudes in these very homes. Because his influence then—twenty or thirty years ago—was limited to *these* homes and had not spread into the general community, we are now seeing the products of *these* homes. Later on we may see more and more young men and women like this from other kinds of families.

At that time the parents in these homes did not want to subject their children to the same traumata to which they had been exposed. On a strong basis of Freudian psychoanalytic theory it was generally felt—and, in fact, still is—that most people's problems stem from a lack of parental love and affection and too harsh a parental attitude about restrictions of freedom, sexual and otherwise. With this in mind parents went out of their way to be affectionate, demonstrative, indulgent of the child's needs and very permissive about his behavior, sexual and otherwise. No big issues were raised about cleanliness or masturbation. The children were given special lessons in swimming, music, dance, to develop their intellectual interests and promote their explorations of their own bodies and minds.

In many ways these child-rearing methods worked. These young men are very open, friendly, get on easily with people, have wholesome relationships with their male peers and with the opposite sex. They are warm, loving, and lovable. They are not anxious about sex or about being liked and accepted by people. They expect to be well-liked and have none of the social or sexual anxieties that so many people had in their parents' generation. So far, so good. So "Spock" worked. Yes, it did work and very well. Except that there is a fly in the ointment. These young men do not seem to be able to choose a profession, to earn a decent living, to channel their considerable intellectual ability and talents into some meaningful career. They come to us therapists lost and floundering. They are still emotionally and financially supported by their parents. They feel defeated by their inability to cope with the challenges of carving a niche for themselves in the world. Now I am not talking about their not being doctors or lawyers or businessmen or any other "establishment" type of "success." They also cannot "put it together" to become poets or rock musicians or graphic artists or athletes if they happen to be talented in these areas. They seem to lack the stick-to-it-iveness or the drive, the will to succeed in *whatever* area it may be. The problem is that *they* are bothered by this. If they were not bothered by it, it would not be a problem for them subjectively. But, in fact, they view themselves as failures, as "gutless," as "cop-outs." They want some of the advantages that ac-

crue from professional and financial success, but they
realize they do not have the *emotional* wherewithal necessary to achieve this.

What happened? How did their upbringing fail them?
It seems to have failed them in that they were presented
with a situation optimal for furthering their emotional
growth, but one that was essentially devoid of hardships,
deprivations, and challenges that they would have had to
fight to overcome. Because of this, they never developed
the particular kind of strength necessary for meeting such
challenges. That strength is what is essential to the
achievement of success in any area—not just the "establishment" kinds of career. So these young men have a
missing part, especially in our society. And this is the
society in which they are living—and will have to function as failures or successes, or at least *function* at all.
Because their parents (or at least one of them) were successful and still serve as models for them, they cannot
easily "drop out" and say that this is a better way of living
life. These boys have usually tried drugs but are not particularly "into" them in a big way. Many have managed
to do fairly well in a scholastic situation—often with all
kinds of help from tutors and with a great deal of cheating. Sometimes if their scholastic course is vigorous, they
fail at this point. Sometimes when it is relatively unchal-
lenging for them, they get through this and then have
trouble after graduation.

It is clear why the syndrome is still sex-linked. In our
society—at least until now—a young woman could avoid
the challenges of a career by getting married, having children, running a house while her husband goes out to a job.
A young man cannot do the equivalent of this in any way
that is generally acceptable socially.

I do not mean that a woman can solve her problems in
this way. Rather it is just that these women have not as
yet made their way to psychoanalysts' offices. I will describe some of these women subsequently. Many of them
have feelings of insecurity and are very frightened of pursuing career goals in any meaningful way. However, they
can and do rationalize that they choose instead to have

children and rear them. Granted this is a rationalization for some of them, but it is one that they can use with some superficial success. Nonetheless the avoidance of developing themselves costs them tremendously in self-esteem, and they never regard themselves as adults who have learned to cope and to take care of themselves and beyond that to be able to express their true creative potential in whatever manner they choose. They feel trapped by their need to be supported.

Getting back to the young men, they are extremely *difficult* for us therapists to treat. The ordinary classical analytic conflicts are not necessarily the main issues for them. What success I have had comes from getting them in touch with their anger at their parents for presenting them with what was essentially a false picture. The parents were not being real and honest with them. They were playing a *role* of being "Spock" parents instead of being depriving, destructive, demanding, frustrating, hostile, as well as loving—in short, all the sides of being human, negative as well as positive. The parents promised them a rose garden where there was just an ordinary field that included a good many weeds.

Instead of producing successful if inhibited, sexually frustrated, socially anxious, compulsive adults in their own image, these parents produced warm, open, friendly, loving, delightful offspring—but lacking the wherewithal to meet the challenges required for success in our society. It is not that Spock was wrong or his child-rearing methods were wrong. *The methods succeeded in the areas in which they were meant to succeed.* It is just that there was that little fly in the ointment—a by-product that was not reckoned with, perhaps could not have been reckoned with then.

At this point, we should add to our orientation for child-rearing the fact that perhaps it is more important for a parent to be totally real and totally honest about his or her feelings than it is for him or her to be consistently loving and permissive.

I have found myself telling these parents that they must change their orientation about what is good and what is bad for their children. Sometimes they have to give themselves points when they frustrate their young adult children and demerits when they indulge them. I have to convince them to refrain from giving their children money, to try to show them that indulgent giving is very destructive to their children and keeps them from growing up.

As individual analytic therapy does not deal at all effectively with these issues, a psychiatrist must judge whether they are the patient's paramount problem. If they are, they can often be dealt with best in a therapy group that includes many people who are unlike these patients. The other people will act as a kind of force of reality and will frequently confront the patient with his evasions, immaturity, and failure to cope. In fact this has happened to patients of this type that I have had in group. It is furthermore important in individual therapy and in group that the therapist does not continue the parental role of an indulgent, permissive "good guy." With these patients especially, but perhaps with almost all patients, the therapist should be real. He ought to express negative as well as positive feelings rather than merely fit the role of a supportive figure who has no personality of his own. There has been a very gradual but definite movement in the field toward the therapist's assuming a more authentic role in relation to his patients, rather than the traditional "blank screen" role. There are some therapists who do not accept the validity of this change, but increasing numbers are moving in that direction.

I want to include here a statement on permissive child-rearing from one of my patients:

"I want to add some thoughts on therapy and Spocked kids. I speak on the basis of five years of therapy and twenty-seven years of Spock childhood.

"I suppose every kind of patient can find ways to use therapy itself to perpetuate his symptoms. Still, this seems peculiarly likely for patients from permissive homes. After all, Spock and traditional psychoanalytic therapy both grow from the same Freudian soil. Both, roughly speaking, try to counteract excess repression by encouraging feeling, pleasure and self-expression. Many Spock parents are themselves therapists or friends of therapists. We, their children, are raised to expect therapy to be the standard next step after college, if we haven't already begun long before that. In other generations, entering psychotherapy was an independent choice, possibly supported by peers, but very likely incomprehensible to parents. For us, it is another stage of childhood.

"Often following the collapse of other values, our parents built their lives around us. They set themselves to serve our needs completely. We were tiny giants, swathed in a dream of lifelong Eden. The world was soft and nourishing, with us at the center. We barely began to cry or complain and food was on the way.

"We were carefully protected from the consequences of our own actions. For example, I knew that if I lost any money, my father would give it right back to me. It was only fair. At eight or nine I realized that my mother just couldn't make me cry: her anger was unconvincing. I knew she would back down in any fight because at heart she wanted me to win. Then she could praise me for being so forceful and determined. When I really needed determination, say in building a tricky model airplane, I got the message that only a fool (later on—a masochist) would put up with so much frustration.

"Thank God that college takes many of us away from home. Maybe by the time we're twenty, reality has intruded enough to shake our faith that the whole world loves us as our parents did. Where's our attentive audience? Why can't they see how important we are? There must be a trick.

"We imagine ourselves as magical Peter Pan angel artists. Or better yet, World Saviors—rock musicians remaking the universe with a million amp twitch, Tim Leary tweaking everyone's DNA, or my friend David who will be Omnipotent Pope Emperor Che Mao Lord Christ Gautama of the Universe or nothing, zero, null. So he can't get it together to make a career as World Savior. He just can't get those graduate school applications in the mail.

"Then we find a doctor who, if he is more or less traditional, leads us back into dreams and the past. It's easy and it holds out magical promise—change your head and the world is yours. (We see it that way even if his pitch is more modest.) If we have some of the old hang-ups of repression, we may make real progress on them without ever touching the fundamental unreality. We are traveling inward to fantasy and distortion instead of outward to a reality where our actions can be truly reflected. We are only delaying the moment when we will have to take reality seriously, frustrations and all. When you don't have any sense of scale, when you don't know if you're the size of an ant or a galaxy, dreaming a lot won't straighten you out.

"You need an accurate mirror. For me, carpentry work has helped. Wood takes a saw-cut where you put it. The boards don't leap off the floor and shape themselves into a table at your wish. The wood resists, but it's finally tractable if you're patient. It doesn't lie to you. That is surely one reason why so many of us have taken to crafts, car repair, farming.

"Within conventional treatment, a group is better than individual therapy. The Spock child is the power center of his family. His parents are there to serve his needs. Individual therapy recreates the peculiar situation in which another person gives you his complete attention. No matter what you talk about, this situation can't help you take your own measure. The problem is compounded if your parents are paying the bills for this exclusive attention. In contrast, group therapy brings you face-to-face with the fact that you are just one of many.

"For the same reason, I have grown almost grateful that I had an angry (non-Spock) older brother to break the enchanted circle of my family. I also begin to feel grateful that I went to conventional public schools and a college where I had to meet definite standards. Spock children who attend certain kinds of schools may never face any hard demands at all. One graduate from the progressive high school where I teach returned to complain, 'Back here I was loved just as I was. I never really had to produce— I never really had to grow.' Of course, the answer is not to turn the school into a factory, but to insist on some clear and realistic demands.

"Some of my students have arrived at another answer

which may have wider importance. Borrowing in part from the Chinese, they have developed communal education classes in which all members participate as equals and the group evaluates each individual's work. They use the group's conscience to reinforce their own desire to be productive and the results have been good—they are more able to do what they want to do.

"We Spock kids were raised in a murky cocoon where nothing was definite except our own transcendent importance. Our best hope seems to lie in confronting firm realities outside our own heads."

These young men in treatment with me (and with many of my colleagues) are merely the tip of the iceberg. There appears to be a general dissatisfaction even within the intellectual community with the results of our current methods of child-rearing. Twenty or thirty years ago, parents at least felt comfortable in the illusion that they knew what the best way to raise a child was. The prevalent psychoanalytic ideas in the late forties (and indeed since then, except in some circles that have become more questioning) had their emphasis on Freud's instinct theory. To put it in an admittedly simplistic way, people were thought to generate certain drives—sexual, anal and oral. The thwarting of the expression and the gratification of these drives was supposedly what led people to be neurotic. Therefore, it seemed and indeed it was very logical to assume that correct child-rearing should involve helping the child to gratify these drives with the least possible interference from parents. So being an enlightened parent in those days (and I must freely admit that I myself was one of them) meant that I had to try to decipher what my child seemed to need or wish to express, put my own needs and interests as much in the background as possible, and help the child gratify the need. This was thought to be almost as true for age three months as it was for age three years as it was for age thirteen. When I was selfish and tried to get my own needs gratified in opposition to my child's, I felt guilty. When I put my child ahead of myself, I felt I was a good parent.

Now since those days there has been a tremendous explosion of knowledge about child development in the field of psychoanalysis. I will go into this in greater detail in a subsequent chapter. But very, very briefly, some of the work on what is called Object Relations has pointed out the enormous need for a very close consistent relationship to a mother during the first year or two of life. Any separation at that point, even a brief one, is extremely traumatic to a child. Along with these discoveries there have been others in a field called Ego Psychology, which show that after the first couple of years, a child *needs* to separate and individuate from his mother, to get a very clear feeling of the difference between his needs and wishes and those of his mother. His mother not only must let him go away from her as much as is consistent with his age, but must present herself as a separate personality with her own "selfish" needs, not just as an extension of the child that fulfills *his* needs. This is an obviously and admittedly simplistic summary of the last twenty-five years of progress in psychoanalytic theory. However, it can be seen that just these two discoveries have very serious implications for child-rearing that are quite different from our earlier views. They also tend to raise some questions about issues like day-care centers for very young children, about shared child-rearing between both parents, and about some of our modern educational methods. It may be that the theories on which some of these ideas are based are now outmoded and incorrect. Some of these theoretical issues and their application in specific areas will be dealt with in subsequent chapters.

When I have discussed these new views or written about them, there have usually been certain general objections or disagreements raised that I should like to bring up myself now and discuss. One of the most consistent objections to my point of view was that I was interested in producing successful young adults who fit into the requirements of our society. What was wrong with producing a generation of beautiful, warm, open, loving people who had no big social or sexual problems? Why did I care whether they were establishment successes? Why did *I* describe them as "gutless cop-outs?" Did *I* want to produce automatons who would fit into our society of exploitative, dishonest, war-mongering people? My answer to that is that *I* did not set up any standards for these young people to meet. *They* came to see me. I did not solicit them. They were dissatisfied with not coming up to their *own* ego-ideal. They were dismayed at their inability to attain their own goals, no matter how little or how much these goals were socially acceptable. I too deplore a child-rearing system that produces adults that conform to a society. There should be instilled in a well-raised person the ability to disagree and to produce changes that can help a society or, failing that, even the ability to drop out of a society but with the inner conviction and peace of mind to accept this decision with dignity and self-esteem. These young people are not happy with *themselves*. They feel crippled. They lack their own direction. They are goalless and rudderless, but not happy at being this way. Their upbringing has not made them happy with themselves. They are unable to live up to society's standards or their own, to drop out because *they* decide to or stay in because they want to.

Another objection from some of my younger critics has been the argument that their quarrel is with the society, this society which I feel kids have to learn to cope with realistically. They insist that since the society is in many instances clearly wrong—either unjust or inconsistent with real human needs—why should they learn to deal with it; they want to change it. But that is a real factor in what I am saying: these kids, reared in this unchallenged, inauthentic manner, will not have the capacity, the will, the ability to change society if indeed they want to do so! They may well be right: there are many things about our society that need alteration, but it requires strength of purpose, dedication, the ability to deal with disappointments, an understanding of the reality of people and our world, to change that world! Those who cannot "get it together" even to keep a non-establishment job for six months or to find one, will not be able to change the world.

Another corollary to this point of view is the argument that I am advocating a return to discipline—to the old "spare the rod and spoil the child" philosophy. Here too, my real beliefs appear to have little to do with this argument against them. I am looking for *authenticity* in a parent, not for a disciplinarian. But, in fact, if a parent's more natural bent is to exert discipline, and he is pulling himself out of shape not to do this because he feels it will harm his child, it might be important for him to know he may be doing *more* harm by being inauthentic.

To sum up, many discoveries in the field of child development over the past twenty-five years have not been clearly incorporated into our theories of child-rearing. These discoveries as well as some of the results of our operating under the old theories have brought the latter into question. Perhaps we are ready for a revision in our views of child-rearing, a major revision rooted both in theoretical discoveries and in the failures in our expectations from the use of the old theoretical model. I certainly do not in any way advocate throwing out the baby with the bath water. Some of the old changes along the lines of greater permissiveness in the areas of toilet training, masturbation, and sexuality in general appear to me to have held up very well and produced the desired results. They should certainly be reinforced rather than revised. However, other ideas have not held up. They are the ones we must examine and question and decide how to modify.

SOME THEORY:
RECENT RESEARCH IN THE PSYCHOANALYTIC VIEW OF CHILD DEVELOPMENT

In psychoanalysis we are taught that one cannot have an adequate technique without a theory on which it is based. Before embarking on the "how to," the actual techniques of child-rearing, I want to try to give to you very briefly, and admittedly in a grossly inadequate and summary fashion, some of the developments in theory over the past decade or two—since Spock's original book—that might influence our technique in bringing up children. I am certain that ten years from now another such book will have to be written to amend this one. The field of psychoanalysis over the past two decades but perhaps especially over the past ten or fifteen years has had such a tremendous explosion of knowledge that no analyst of any merit could be recognized today from the way he practiced ten years ago. Knowledge of theory accumulates and brings about marked changes in the technique we use to deal with patients. Some of these same changes in theory, I believe, have marked implications for our ways of bringing up our children. In this chapter I will try to give you in as non-technical a manner as possible what I believe to be the major recent developments in the field of psychoanalytic theory that have practical application to child-rearing.

Let us start off at the beginning. Birth constitutes quite a traumatic event for babies. There is a short period of oxygen lack which gives them their first experience of anxiety. Also infants must make a tremendous change in their way of being, going from a parasite in the uterus to a state in which they are completely helpless and dependent on the outside world to fulfill their needs. However, at birth they are unable to any great extent to tell the difference between what is internal and part of their own body and what is external to them. Newborns generally express discomfort with the change they are experiencing over the first few days.

In the period following birth, and almost as a reflex, when the infant's mouth is stimulated, his head moves toward the stimulating force and his mouth snaps. This response lasts for two months and is present only when he is hungry. In this phase the infant has for a long time been thought to have no *clear* visual or auditory perceptions of people, though he can respond to direct physical contact. In this phase shortly after birth the infant cries not really in order to communicate with his mother, but rather to relieve tension created by being cold or hungry. However, the mother's response to this cry gradually begins to mean to the baby that the cry can be used as a communication to another person. But for the newborn the world around him holds no particular interest because he does not perceive it as a possible source of satisfaction. He himself is his main source of satisfaction. He basically cannot see or hear very well and is aware only of himself and his own body.

Very recent work that has not been conclusively proven or generally accepted as yet but is nonetheless extremely suggestive tends to show that even a newborn is able to distinguish different visual and auditory stimuli. In other words even a newborn baby can *to some degree* see and hear. And newborns appear to have different kinds of responses to their mother's face and voice than they do to other stimuli even during the *first few days of life:* so not only can they see and hear but they can discriminate. Some studies seem to indicate that their world is even three-dimensional. They have different responses to two- and three-dimensional forms and to their mother's face as contrasted with other faces; this differentiation occurs as early as two weeks of age. This new work opens up a whole new world to understanding and explaining why traumata in the mother-child relationship that occur even right after birth can have such a profound effect.

Along the lines of this research there appear to be different responses in newborns who spend a great deal of time with their mothers (as would be the case in primitive societies) versus newborns in a hospital who either because of illness or prematurity in themselves or simply because of hospital routine are only with their mothers briefly and at intervals. Many hospitals have routines that involve total separation of mother and child for forty-eight hours after birth followed by four-hourly reunions. Apparently when something interferes with the mother-child interaction even in the first days of life, observable effects can persist for many months if not longer. A difference has even been noted at both thirty weeks and sixty weeks between babies whose mothers have had certain anesthetics during labor and those whose mothers have not. Those whose mothers had the drug are less closely involved in interchanges with their mothers and show more self-stimulating activities like thumb-sucking. No evidence of consequences past the first year has been accumulated to date; however, such consequences are certainly possible, even probable.

Other studies have shown that breast-feeding mothers tend to feed their babies more frequently than bottle-feeding mothers and to fit their feeding to the baby's need rather than other factors. Breast-feeding thus tends to reduce further the separation between mother and child. The general findings by these researchers seem to indicate that mothers who breast feed are more apt to have a closer interaction with and less separation from their babies.

Between the eighth and the twelfth weeks the infant begins to be able to see better. So now a world out there beyond his own boundaries comes gradually into being. Toward the latter part of the second month the infant begins to be able to distinguish clearly another human being, though this occurs only when he is hungry. During the third month the infant can follow a grown-up's face with his eyes. The sight of the face becomes a symbol to the baby for the relief of tension in himself. From the third to the sixth month the baby begins to smile when the face is presented in such a way that it can be seen straight on and is moving in some way. At this time the baby will respond to the face with a smile whereas it will *not* respond with a smile to a bottle of milk. The baby is now able to distinguish a part of its environment that is especially meaningful to him from the rest of the environment.

During the second half of the first year the baby becomes able to recognize the mother, and sometimes the father too, as a whole person even when he does not need to be fed. This represents a shift from his merely seeing her as satisfying a need to be fed to his deriving pleasure from being with another person. Between six and eight months the baby can distinguish between different people. He generally will refuse to make contact with a stranger. He will cover his eyes or his face or turn away and evince a certain amount of anxiety. This is called "the eighth-month anxiety" and is evidence that he has fixed on his mother as the specific person he "loves." At the beginning of the third month the mother may be split into a good mother when she gratifies the baby's needs and a bad one when she does not. Toward the end of the first year she is no longer split in the baby's mind. All through this phase the mother is enormously important to the child and has the potential of making every experience a good or a bad one. During this period the mother's presence provides a great deal of security and also offers the child a model to imitate and identify with. The social patterns between the mother and child in the second half of the first year contain the basic elements for the development of the child's social relationships throughout life. That is why the presence of a good loving mother is so essential during this period. When the child is going through his "eighth-month anxiety," if he has an essentially loving mother his hostile impulses, generated by her leaving him at times and her not gratifying his needs immediately, are modified by his experience of her coming back after leaving him and her being consistently loving and caring. If the mother is *not* present or *not* loving, his destructive impulses are not neutralized, and they may well be directed against other people or against himself throughout his life. As seen above, some sort of preverbal communication is established between mother and child even in the very first months of life and even before the child can actually perceive the mother. It is part of an instinctual psychobiological response. That is the reason why disturbances or disruptions in the mother-child relationship even in the first weeks of life can have extremely profound effects.

During nursing the child responds strongly to the mother's presence and her attitude rather than her words. During the second half of the first year of life or when the baby is crawling or walking, the mother begins to say "No" and to shake her head to prevent the child from doing certain things. The child understands the meaning of this verbal symbol and its physical head-shaking accompaniment. He begins to imitate the mother and now has an important symbol himself through which he can convey a feeling. When his mother says "No" to him, the child is caught up in a conflict between his "love" for his mother and his anger at her for frustrating him. He has to choose between the discomfort of yielding to her commands and the fear of losing her love. One solution he finds is to identify with the person who is frustrating him and to become the "No" sayer himself. This is one of the first signs of the beginning of his *autonomy* and his being able to distinguish between *self* and *other*. This usually occurs between the twelfth and fifteenth month. The evolution of the relationship between mother and child requires a continuous open communication of feelings between them. The image the child has of himself as a *self* grows out of a continued interaction with mother as well as an identification with her. Sometimes because of her own emotional difficulties, the mother is unable to perceive the child's emotional needs. Sometimes the mother may see the child as an extension of herself and, to give an example, feed the child when *she* in fact is hungry. Though some mothers appear to be devoted to their children, their constant controls and intrusions are a sign that they are unable to establish clear boundaries and separation between themselves and the child. This produces a situation in which the child fails to trust his own signals and may give up trying to communicate. This same problem can be brought about by parents who lie or distort the truth or hide some fact or feeling. Then the child may begin to mistrust either his mother's words or his own ability to comprehend them. Since words from this point on become a major method of communicating, this distortion in their use by the parent can have profound effects on the child's ability to communicate with others and to trust his own perceptions. This applies especially to promises. If promises are not kept, then the child's ability to predict what will occur, through reliance on the belief in words, may be impaired. The verbal interaction between parent and child cannot be overestimated as a precursor of the child's ability to relate to others throughout his life.

The image a child has of his own body (in distinction from the intellectual or objective view he may have of it) grows out of many complex components including the sensations he experiences from the different parts of his body plus looking at his body parts plus the experience of looking in the mirror. This mirror phase goes on from about the age of eight months to as late as fifteen months and gradually enables the child to experience his body as a whole rather than as a sum of different parts. But in addition to the real mirror, in a subjective sense his mother's face is a mirror. It is very important, especially during the first year and a half of his life, when his image of his body is being formed, that he see adoration and adulation in the face of his mother as she looks at him. Psychoanalytic theory during the past ten years has focused a great deal of attention on the need a child has for this adoring parental response. We are now aware that some of the defects in body-image or the excessive need to focus on the body that we see later are the result of the lack of such a response.

When a baby is entirely dependent on the mother, he needs to be held a great deal. I mean this literally. But when I say "hold him very very close," I also mean that the baby's total environment must create the effect of stability, of holding and supporting him. The phrase "good enough mothering" has been coined to describe mothering that basically fulfills the infant's needs. Physical holding may be the only way a mother can communicate love to her baby during the first months of life. However, it is not only the act of being held that is important to the child, but also the *quality* of the holding. A "good enough" mother not only instinctively and intuitively responds with caring, but also gradually allows the infant to experience an ever-increasing amount of frustration. The mother's gradual weaning of the child from her breast is one part of this, but weaning must be interpreted in a much broader way than the mere cessation of breast-feeding. Maternal care has to be defined not only in objective terms but in the amount of subjective pleasure and joy that the mother derives from the experience. The mother must not only protect the baby but must gradually expose him to experiences in which he does not get everything he wants the moment he wants it. The child's ability to deal with reality is determined by this. Problems in this pattern of development can occur when the mother's emotional difficulties interfere, when there are excessive separations from the mother, or when she is faced with a particularly difficult task due to severe physical illness or congenital or hereditary defects in the child. However, when the development proceeds well, the mother has been protective enough when the baby needed protection and then intuitive enough at the proper time to allow him to face *gradually* the realities of frustration. In this case the child develops a healthy sense of self and of separateness from the mother. Coinciding with this, the mother must also be able to wean herself away from the child.

The weaning process teaches the child to experience and to handle his anxiety and aggression: the frustration and very gradual deprivation produces anxiety and anger, but in small doses that the child learns to master little by little. It's not unlike the desensitization process that doctors use with allergic patients, in which very tiny doses of the allergents gradually desensitize the allergic person. Children who have not gone through this process of weaning (and of course I mean figurative as well as literal weaning) are not able to deal with their aggression; often they become rather passive and apathetic.

The initial phase of union between mother and child has been labeled *symbiosis*. This is a term borrowed from botany indicating a situation in which a host plant cannot survive without a parasite and conversely the parasite cannot survive without the host. The relationship between mother and child is normally a symbiotic one until the latter part of the first year when the infant becomes a toddler. This point initiates the development of a new phase called *separation-individuation*. This phase is not threatening to the child (though there is always a certain amount of fear of separation), for along with this separation there is a gradual increase in the child's pleasure in his independent functioning. This phase is crucial to the child's ability to achieve and maintain a sense of identity, individuality, and autonomy. Sometimes in the process of going from symbiosis to separation a "transitional object" is used. This is an object like a pillow or blanket or teddy bear that the child has endowed with some of the feelings he has experienced with his mother.

The mother's role in the phase of separation requires a great sensitivity to the balance between the child's emotional needs and his ability to tolerate frustration. Also not all children are the same. Some have needs that are gratified easily and they can also accept frustrations easily. Some are tense, hyperactive and difficult either to nurture or to frustrate. The success of the separation-individuation process depends on the particular dovetailing or lack of it between the mother's personality and the child's genetic and constitutional endowment. The first signs of individuation can be seen as early as the fourth month with crawling. The process gains momentum in the second half of the first year and continues from there. And at first, the child needs to return to the mother frequently for "refueling" after venturing off on his own.

When a mother is absent during the first year of life of a child, his physiological as well as his psychological development will be profoundly affected. First, because of his helplessness, his needs for food and warmth must be provided for by the environment. In addition, aside from these basic physiological needs, a child requires some psychological gratifications. A good example of this is the need for sucking. But a child also requires a give and take with another human being that is provided by the mother's touching him, talking and singing to him, and rocking him. He also requires an environment that is stable and protective. The mother needs to be flexible and responsive to the baby's needs rather than to externally determined schedules. It is important that deprivation is defined as withholding not merely life and death needs but also psychological necessities.

Studies have been made of babies who had relatively good relationships with their mothers during the first six months of their lives but were then separated from them without an adequate replacement for a period of three months. Whereas the babies had been happy before the separation, they became weepy, then withdrawn, then began to lose weight and show a susceptibility to infections. After some months their normal development was impaired, the weepiness stopped, and they developed rigid expressions and a lack of interest in their environment. Separations such as this after a good period of six months previously can be at least partially reversed if the mother returns within a period of three to five months. Even here there may well be some irreversible effects. However if the emotional deprivation continues more than five months, a state of physical and mental deterioration follows that may well lead to death. Even if the child survives, the effects are irreversible. These effects include overall regression of motor development, eye coordination and ability to communicate. If the deprivation continues (and I am talking about children whose needs for food and warmth and medical care are provided), then rocking and strange finger movements appear. Problems in breathing and in digestion manifest themselves and the child is susceptible to infection. A very high death rate is reported. But even in cases of very mild deprivation, psychological development can be seriously affected. The child's ability to use his intelligence is impaired; there is retardation in speech, passivity toward social contacts or new stimuli, and at times anti-social behavior. The child's ability to love may be damaged irreversibly. The earlier in life the emotional deprivation is experienced the more marked its effects. Maximum effects occur if the deprivation took place in the first six months of life and are greater when the infant originally had a good relationship with his mother. The longer the period of emotional deprivation the greater its consequences. Of course, maternal deprivation can occur with a mother constantly present physically but unable to respond emotionally to her child. This is more likely to occur in broken or very disturbed homes with absent or psychologically ill fathers. Later on in life, children who have experienced this kind of deprivation have a constant feeling of frustration and either a tremendous craving for affection or an apparent indifference. A distinction must be made between *frustration*, which may aid a child's development, and deprivation, which creates a basic defect in development from which a person never totally recovers.

Studies have shown that the child's "love" for the father has certain differences from his love for the mother. In his "love" for the mother the child starts out by expecting to be gratified entirely: the child is not able to tolerate *any* reason for the mother's absence or lack of response. The "love" for the father has more elements of reality and expectation of frustration in it. This is probably because, in our culture, the relationship with the father develops at a later age and at a time when many of the essential problems have already been worked through in the mother-child relationship.

Some psychoanalysts have attempted to show a correlation between the particular patterns of feeding and weaning children and their personality formation. Those who have had happy and secure feeding and weaning experiences have been found to be optimistic, confident and friendly. Others with unpleasant experiences have been found to be envious, dependent, hostile, impatient and excitable. To me this appears a bit simplistic but there is probably more than a germ of truth in it.

I have attempted the impossible task of trying to summarize some of the salient points in psychoanalytic theory and research over the past decade or two. I have focused especially on the development of the child during his first year of life. That is because much of the research and development of theory has in fact been about this period and also because this material is the most pertinent for this particular book on child-rearing. What happens in the first year of life is very much a prototype for what will happen later. This, I think, we shall see by dealing specifically with different issues in child-rearing.

HOW TO HOLD THEM VERY CLOSE, THEN LET THEM GO:
THE SPECIFICS OF CHILD-REARING

By this time it is almost a truism that appears in every book on child-rearing that parents should not follow any suggestions that do not seem or feel natural to them. As a matter of fact many people believe that one of the disasters of the past twenty-five years is that parents were made to feel insecure about their spontaneous directions in child-rearing, were induced to give up their independence, and became the puppets of psychologists and others who thought they had all the answers. Obviously this is one of my main theses. The whole idea behind this book began with my observations of young adults who were brought up by these kinds of parents. Now it is true no one really made these parents do anything or induced them to follow any particular rules. And it is also true that all the good books on child-rearing always had statements such as: "Don't ever do anything that does not feel right." Nevertheless the total impact of these books was very much in the direction of neglecting this warning and taking the other parts of the book as gospel. This was hardly the fault or the intention of the authors, but in many cases it certainly worked out that way.

Nevertheless, this is just what I am doing, writing another book on "how to raise your children!" For one thing, I believe a book must be written to counteract the effects of the other books. Strangely enough I wrote a similar

25

book about sex, called *Sexual Fulfillment and Self-Affirmation,* about ten years ago to try to counter all of the books teaching sexual technique. That book seems even more pertinent after another decade of books on sexual technique, which in my opinion destroy the essence of sex. So this book, similarly, has as one of its main functions the counteracting of previous books. And probably as soon as it is published, there will be other books written to counteract its import. But aside from counteracting past advice, I think too that there have been significant advances in our understanding of child development that can suggest some very broad outlines and directions in child-rearing. Interestingly enough many of them appear to emphasize the importance of each parent's "doing his own thing"— being spontaneous and following his or her own feelings in child-rearing.

While this book also tells parents what to do and includes the usual admonition to be spontaneous and not do anything that does not feel right, there is a difference in emphasis—hopefully. Other books told you what to do by the numbers and then included (like the Surgeon General's warning on the pack of cigarettes) that following this might be injurious to you and your child's health. This book will try to give a clear theoretical rationale to encourage you to "do your thing" and not follow anyone's advice by the numbers, including mine. This will not merely be stuck in as an afterthought, but reemphasized constantly throughout each aspect of the book. In other words, the main reason for this book is to try to get parents to be themselves, to be authentic, and to convince them that that happens to be best for their child. It helps your child to become a separate person, which is the goal of "letting them go."

Incidentally, perhaps I should clarify what I mean by "separate." By this I do not mean that they will totally cut off from you and you will never see them again as they grow up. I am referring to their being individual, autonomous people. If they do not achieve independence, they may not be bound to you either. But hopefully if they have a good relationship with you, they will *want* to be with you out of choice because they love you and enjoy the time they spend with you and the good parental responses they get from you which they will continue to cherish through their adult lives. Actually being this kind of parent practically assures a continuing relationship with children. Binding children to you may "work" in a way, though the children's contact with you on this basis will be filled with duty and obligation and hardly satisfying for parent or adult child. What may and often does happen is that children who have been bound in this way rebel by totally cutting off the parents who have set up this situation. They come to realize through therapy or otherwise that a continuation of this kind of "binding" relationship is destructive to them and they realize correctly that it is too late to change the pattern; it is better for them to break off the relationship completely.

Now is telling parents to be themselves like putting a loaded gun in the hands of a maniac and giving him a license to kill? Don't some parents need to be restrained and restricted? Can some parents be utterly destructive to their children if they are given license to be themselves? The answer to these questions is obviously yes. There is a small percentage of parents like this. But I am not worried about inciting them to mayhem because the chances that *those* parents would read *this* book are infinitesimal. If you are reading this book, that very fact means that you are a concerned parent who wants to do well by his child and that your natural bent is not toward destructiveness.

With this general introduction, imploring you to follow your own intuition rather than my advice, I will give you some broad areas of ideas about child-rearing while always encouraging you not to follow them blindly. For one thing, these ideas are already being superseded by other and sometimes contradictory ideas. Your feelings in any specific situation are based on a first-hand intimate knowledge of your own, your mate's, and your child's uniqueness which in any given situation might make the general advice all wrong. You know yourself and your child better than any doctor or any book can. Children differ from one another constitutionally and genetically.

Even right after birth, before any major exposure to the environment, these differences are apparent. Some children are passive and quiet; others are active and noisy. Ideas about rearing children must vary, therefore, from child to child as well as from parent to parent. One thing you parents should never give up to anyone else is your autonomy—your total responsibility for your life and your decisions, your right to be wrong, your refusal to conform. In many ways this is the greatest gift you can give your child: the model of a truly unique, independent individual, yourself, with your faults and your strengths. The feeling of being this autonomous individual, of identifying and responding to one's own unique inner self is probably more closely at the core of mental health than any other single issue.

One of the thoughts that may run through your mind as you read this book (especially if you tend to agree with its points of view) is that you may have unwittingly made mistakes in rearing your children. Now what? Well, first of all, try not to feel guilty. Guilt is a destructive emotion that accomplishes absolutely nothing positive. As I will repeat frequently in this book, I made many of the same mistakes that you did. You and I did the best we could, using the prevailing ideas of the time. Many of the theories behind this book were not even well known or disseminated in sophisticated psychoanalytic circles earlier than ten years ago. And their application to bringing up children has not been adequately conceptualized, documented, or widely spread even yet. So you can hardly blame yourself for not knowing what to do when I myself was not only bringing up my own children incorrectly but advising others to do so until fairly recently.

Aside from trying not to feel guilty, is there anything you can do to reverse past mistakes? Suppose you did not hold your baby very, very close? Suppose you let him cry at night as an infant, or went back to work when he was only a few months old, or fed him on a rigid schedule, or took an extended trip without him when he was only one year old? Is there anything you can do about it now to make up for it? The answer, sadly, is no. One of the emphases in this book is the age-specific nature of the child's needs. Being with your child constantly when he is three or four or ten will not only *not* make up for his not being held close enough at age one, it will keep him from "letting go" now, which is what he should be doing at this later age. Being permissive about discipline with him at age eight will certainly not reverse the rigidity you may have used in toilet training him at age two. He needs a firm structure at age eight. So try to do what needs to be done now. Early mistakes cannot be reversed by later ones.

At whatever age your child has reached when you read this book, you must start applying the ideas that are appropriate to that age level. You cannot go back and undo the past; you should go forward from the present.

On the other hand, if you are still involved with your young child in some of these early matters, and you agree with my point of view, by all means change your way of doing things. Yes, it may confuse the child at first, but he will very quickly, and very happily, adjust to a system that hopefully is better for him.

Even after your child's first few years have passed, you may be involved, with the best of intentions, in behavior that tends to bind him to you and retard the "letting go" process. You may be trying to guess what you think will be good for the child and thus act in a stereotyped rather than a genuinely authentic way. You may be abdicating your parental role in discipline. If this is the case, better late than never. Change your position. Explain to this older child the reason for the change. Even though the past cannot be reversed, there is no reason for compounding mistakes by continuing them based on the rationale that a change will confuse the child. Or that admitting your mistake will diminish you in his eyes so greatly that he will lose respect for you. Say to him in an honest, straightforward manner—if he is past three and has therefore some degree of understanding—"I think I've been handling the business [let's say] of your allowance incorrectly. I read a book on it that makes sense to me. So from now on you'll get fifty cents a week. I don't think it's a good idea for you to have to run to me and ask me for money every time you want to buy bubble gum." Rather than being confused or upset, your child will probably be delighted. Of course he may not be quite so delighted when you say to him, "I can't stand rock music, so when I'm home, you will not play it anymore in the living room — only in your own room and not loud enough for me to hear." However, in the long run, it will be helpful to him that you asserted your authentic point of view in a firm, clear manner. And *you* will not be so angry at him for having made you suffer the music that you scream at him when he steps on your toe by accident! Both giving him his own allowance and telling him what you really like and want him to do or not to do are authentic ways of helping him grow up to be an independent human being.

In general the answer to the question about undoing mistakes seems something like the excellent motto of Alcoholics Anonymous. Accept what you cannot change—what is already past and unable to be changed because it was a time-specific thing. Change what you can change—what is still in the process of happening. And try to be wise enough to tell which is which.

Incidentally, in the course of this book I will refer to the child as "he." It is merely expedient not to have to repeat "he or she". But this is not to be construed in any way as anti-female. As a matter of fact, I have written a section specifically on feminism. Before embarking on a discussion of the specifics of child-rearing, I should state my own views on feminism. I am very proud to consider myself a feminist, and I have consistently espoused the cause, even marching down Fifth Avenue in the First Feminist March. I am very much in favor, from many points of view (including what I judge to be best for men), of fathers being as involved as mothers in raising children, practically from birth onward. I do feel that it is important for a child to have a consistent relationship with the mother during the first two years of life. But I understand that this can be done, and is being done, by some energetic and enterprising women without giving up their professional roles and by enlisting the help of their husbands and some other intimate. However, at this point in history, as I write this book, I am gearing it to the reality of the vast majority of families in which, after all, the mother plays the dominant role in child-rearing. This is not necessarily the way I would like it to be; unhappily, that is the way it is for the present. I would be more than happy if this book had to be drastically revised within the next ten years to include a much bigger role for the father.

────────────────────SHOULD YOU HAVE A BABY?

Your autonomy starts right here. In the past in this country and even today in some other countries, lack of knowledge or availability of contraceptive methods did not permit this choice. People had children whether they wanted to or not. This in itself made for a poor milieu for parent-child relationships. A parent was trapped into being a parent. But even after extensive dissemination of knowledge and availability of contraceptive methods, how many people really make a totally clear, thought-out decision *not* to have children? You have to be clear on the total freedom you have *not* to have a child before you can make a clear, positive, and autonomous choice to have a child. You should not have a child to provide your parents with a grandchild. Even after conception, the availability of safe and inexpensive and totally legal abortion makes it possible for you to decide *not* to have a child. The positive decision to have a child should be based on your own and your mate's uniqueness and not on the fact that procreation is a natural instinct or that the world would not go on without it. Both future parents should be involved in the decision. If there is an original disagreement, the decision should not be made without the agreement of both. Tremendous bitterness has been generated by a wife's or husband's unilateral decision to have a child by withholding contraception without the mate's knowledge. The world will go on very well without *your* child. And the world, you, and your mate will probably go on a lot better if you don't have a child that both you and your mate do not very specifically decide to have. Not all people should have children. There are some women and men who find it difficult to relate to a child, who prefer other activities, who are basically unable or unwilling to make the necessary adjustments in their lives that must inevitably occur especially during the early years of a child's life. All of these issues should receive a great deal of serious consideration before a decision is made to have a child. Having a child should *not* be based on following the social pattern of the establishment or the majority of people in the world. It should be a very personal decision —a decision arrived at with your mate and one that you take the full responsibility for making. In this way you will not face being a parent with the feeling that it was something that happened to happen to you. That feeling can lead to resentment and to perceiving the child as an unwanted burden. This applies, of course, not only to the first child but to every subsequent child. An additional child should *not* be conceived because little Johnny needs a baby sister. That may enter into your decision, but *you*, not little Johnny, have the responsibility of making the decision. Don't cop out by putting it on him or asking him what *he* wants. It's totally up to you to decide.

An important part of your decision as to whether or not you should have a baby in the first place should rest on whether you think you could be the kind of parent who has the ability to hold a baby very very close to you in the first year or two of his life *and* the ability to let go of him when he grows older. Do you enjoy holding other people's babies? (Though it's true that some people feel differently about holding other people's babies than they do when they have their own.) Does your particular life-style allow you to spend a great deal of time with the baby during the first years of his life without sacrificing too many of your other interests? Later on will you be able to allow a child to separate from you without subtly subverting and sabotaging his efforts at growth and independence? Are you a possessive person who tends to swallow or dominate others? If your answers are mainly that it is hard for you to hold babies close and then hard to let them go, think twice.

Of course, from a medical point of view including the safety of the mother and the baby, it is almost inevitably best to have the baby in a hospital. This too, though, is a choice that *you* have the responsibility to make. There are different kinds of hospitals. From what we know about very early infantile development, it would seem to me that it is important to go to a place that allows the maximum time for contact between infant and mother from birth on, a place where mothers are allowed to hold them very very close. This means you must pick an obstetrician who is affiliated with such a hospital and who shares your ideas about what is important emotionally during the neo-natal period. You might think that such an obstetrician would be easy to find, but this is not necessarily so. Obstetricians are not generally known for their interest or wisdom about this period. In some ways a peasant who has her baby delivered by a midwife in a one-room hut may be better off in terms of providing a better psychological milieu for developing the close mother-child relationship that is important even during the first week of life than you are in the fanciest, sterilized, super-organized, scientific hospital. Though the infant's sense experience is certainly limited in some ways right after birth, this does not mean that he does not have a total and important emotional response to the presence or absence of mothering.

To my mind the baby's postnatal environment has a profound influence on his later adaptation. If there is ever a most crucial time to hold them very close, it is at this time. I feel that the closer the child is to the mother's body and the longer the time he has this during the postnatal period the better it will be for the child in the long run. The contiguity of skin to skin and the warmth of the mother's body gives the newborn a feeling of safety and security. Even as adults we know how much comfort there can be in having another's body close to ours.

I have had patients whose emotional problems could be

traced back literally to the first *weeks* of their lives. I will give you an example in the subsequent section on feeding.

NATURAL CHILDBIRTH

Whether or not to have natural childbirth is very much a personal decision. Unless you have a doctor who believes strongly in this, a husband who will be happy to go through the preparation for it as well as the delivery with you, and a hospital whose staff will support you, you had better forget about it. Don't feel that you are committing a sin against motherhood or your child if you choose *not* to have it. Whereas for some mothers natural childbirth may be a boon and a tremendously satisfying experience, for others it will result in great pain and suffering with no real reward. Tense women will rarely be able to enjoy the pleasures without too great a payment in pain and discomfort. Too much general anesthesia may produce some subsequent difficulty for the child, but a local or saddle block type of anesthesia has little against it in any way. These types of anesthesia avoid severe pain and avoid the anesthetic going through the blood stream into the baby's system. At the same time they allow the mother to be conscious and able to experience the delivery.

Here, too, be yourself, make your own decision *authentically* based on what *you* want, not what books and articles for or against various forms of childbirth may induce you to feel you ought to do.

FEEDING

One of the earliest decisions that a mother is faced with is whether or not to breast-feed the child. First of all it is important to realize that either way this decision is made is not terribly crucial to the child. Everything else being equal—which it rarely is—purely from the child's point of view it probably is better generally to breast-feed. It insures the kind of physical contact between mother and child, the skin on skin and mouth on nipple contact that gives a great deal of satisfaction and security to a baby when it is provided by a mother who is comfortable and derives satisfaction herself from the process. *But*—the last part of that sentence is the big "but." There are many women who may not particularly like the process, who may need more mobility than breast-feeding allows, who may have a strong narcissistic investment in the beauty of their breasts (look at all the plastic surgery done on breasts today) for whom breast-feeding is a burden and more displeasure than pleasure. For that kind of woman breast-feeding ends up being a disservice to herself and her child. It is the *quality* of the mothering that affects the child. The quality is going to be vastly impaired if a mother does not really want to breast-feed. The child needs a great deal of contact and closeness, but with a mother who enjoys it. Contact and closeness with a mother who is anxious or resentful causes more harm than good. And there can be a good deal of contact and closeness with a mother who holds her baby while the baby is feeding from the bottle. The important thing is that the mother should take the responsibility of making this decision about breast-feeding. She should not leave the decision to her husband, her mother, her doctor, or a book.

If the breast-feeding mother has sufficient milk, most authorities feel it is better for her to use one breast at each feeding. This will allow the baby to get as much sucking as he needs. If the mother uses both breasts, the baby may be full of milk before he has satisfied his need to suck. If the mother does not have enough milk to use just one breast at a feeding, she should keep the baby on one breast for twenty minutes. This way, even though most of the feeding takes place in the first five minutes, the baby will have sufficient sucking.

Even if a mother breast feeds, she should introduce a relief bottle at least twice a week and possibly as often as once a day. This will get the baby accustomed to the bottle in case the mother has to be away and miss an occasional feeding. It will also lessen the trauma of a total abrupt switch to a bottle in case of illness, accident or other unforeseen circumstance.

Feeding experiences even during the first weeks of life can have a very profound influence on a child's emotional development and his subsequent behavior as an adult. I want to report a rare and rather extreme example of this from my practice, not because I want to frighten you, but because I want to impress you with the tremendous import that very early experiences can have on a person.

I saw a twenty-two-year-old man, rescued by the police after he had deliberately lain down in the middle of a heavily traveled road at night in a conscious attempt to kill himself. This had followed a relatively mild argument with his girl friend and an irrational fear on his part that she might leave him. Whenever there was a minor disruption in the emotional contact between him and his girl friend, he would invariably think of suicide, though this had been his first actual attempt. His only other symptom was enuresis (bed-wetting). What struck me as unusual about this young man was that apart from his specific symptoms, he appeared to be the picture of mental health. He related very easily to me, he was friendly, he got along very well with his parents, siblings and peers. He had an excellent sense of his own masculinity, he liked his work and was reasonably productive in it. An extensive history also revealed no specific area of trauma. His father was a bit distant, but not remarkably so. He had an excellent relationship with his mother. There was no obvious clue that could explain his tremendous oversensitivity to his girl friend. And yet, but for a bit of good fortune, he would have been dead—a suicide.

I began treating him by using the psychoanalytic method and encouraging him to remember and report his dreams. He had dream after dream about starving almost to death and anxiety, rage, and despair connected with these experiences. In real life he could connect to no such experiences and the nature of his emotional nurture from his mother was basically consistent and warm and loving. In his dreams his despair at being separated from his girl friend as well as his bed-wetting appeared to be related to a very early experience of being cut off from nourishment from his mother and a rage that was turned against himself in the form of suicide or expressed in an infantile way as bed-wetting. He and I concluded that there must have

been some very early trauma that threatened his very
existence. I asked him to check with his mother. She told
him that when he was *three weeks* old, her milk had apparently diminished in nutriment and that he had screamed
for several days and apparently been on the verge of death
from starvation before this was discovered and subsequently corrected. The analysis of this very early trauma
worked so well that his enuresis and suicidal thoughts
essentially stopped and he was even able to survive his
finding out about his girl friend's infidelity to him at a
subsequent date and go on to marry her and live happily
with her. The reason I give this rather startling case illus-
tration is to emphasize the point that trauma at an extremely early age can have very far-reaching effects on
personality development. An infant may not appear to be
affected by his surroundings but actually he is very much
affected. In fact the earlier the trauma, in general the more
far-reaching the effect.

So, to return to feeding during the first year of life: demand feeding—when the baby wants it—is clearly preferable to schedule feeding. At this time of his life, the baby
requires an environment that gratifies his internal needs.
He is not physically or psychologically prepared to adapt
himself to the demands of outside forces, like waiting to
be fed at the convenience of his mother's timing. When
he is forced to do so, the baby experiences terror of starvation and enormous rage. When these feelings are evoked
beyond a certain degree, the baby must evolve a whole set
of defenses to cope with them. (The term "primal scream"
is a reflection of these feelings and a whole method of
therapy, primal scream therapy, has been evolved by Dr.
Janov in an attempt to reverse this process.)

Most babies, fed on demand, begin to put themselves
on a schedule after a time in any case—a schedule based
on their own evolving physical and psychological needs.
Often, after a time, it resembles the once-every-four-
hours of the scheduled feeding method.

DEMAND FEEDING

SOLID FOODS

Pediatricians vary on the time to introduce solid foods and their advice varies from one baby to another depending on the vicissitudes of his digestive system. Some doctors believe in introducing solid foods even after one month, while others favor waiting till three or even five months. The truth is, these views are often fads and vary from decade to decade. The individual baby's needs are the important thing to consider. If you like and trust your pediatrician, and your baby is generally healthy, you will do best being guided in this matter by his advice.

It is very important for the mother to be sensitive to how much the baby wants and *not* to overfeed. The relationship between mother and child revolves around the feeding situation in the first year; this often influences the patterns of socialization the child will have for the rest of his life. So try to make feeding a pleasant, friendly matter, free from forcing or power struggles.

WEANING

A discussion about weaning must be divided into two parts—weaning from the breast and weaning from the bottle—but there are really few differences between them. Weaning from the breast is certainly one of the first and most important parts of the process of "letting them go." Many mothers get a great deal of emotional (and even, to a certain extent, sexual) gratification from nursing their babies. A part of them will be reluctant to give this up, though another part will respond to the advantages of giving it up in terms of increased freedom and mobility. An important issue then is that weaning should be gradual, not only for the child's sake but for the mother as well. The mechanics of binding breasts, decreasing fluid intake, breast pumps, medications to decrease milk flow are all well covered by other books on baby care, or can be dealt with by a pediatrician. Most experts advise that weaning should be instituted at about five months of age, by offering the baby a sip of milk from a cup and gradually increasing the amount he takes in from it. When he gets enough from the cup, one of the breast feedings can be replaced entirely by a cup feeding; then a little later, an additional cup feeding can replace another breast feeding, and so on. It is usually a good idea to have a baby weaned from the breast by six or seven months. Continuing beyond that is likely to retard the normal "letting go" process.

Sometimes because she is unable to produce milk or is not interested in it, finds it unpleasant, or prefers a greater degree of freedom and mobility, a mother who has begun feeding by the breast may choose to switch from breast to bottle before the usual time for switching to a cup. This can certainly be accomplished at about two months, even one, but it is preferable to wait until three months, to avoid the possibility of colic. Part of the gradual switch is dictated by the mother's discomfort with her breasts as well as the baby's distress over too sudden a change.

Weaning from bottle to cup is not that much different. In general, it should be accomplished about the same time as weaning from the breast and in the same gradual way. It is not a particularly good idea to allow the baby to continue to have the bottle—even at night—beyond six or seven months because it retards the separation process and does not encourage the baby's optimal independent functioning.

PACIFIERS

In addition to feeding, infants need to suck. With this in mind I feel that pacifiers make a good deal of sense and can be very helpful to young children who need them. But again if they personally disgust or horrify you as a parent, for whatever reason, it is obviously better not to use them because your horror will be transmitted to the child and the total experience will do more harm than good.

It does not really make any difference from what issue the parents' disgust with the pacifier originates or whether it is healthy or neurotic or a matter of taste. What matters is that the parent accept his own feelings and deal with this issue in a way that reflects who he is at that point in time rather than who he thinks he should be or who he hopes to become in the future. In the long run the child will be less confused by a parent's being authentic and consistent and by his expressing his real feelings and points of view than he will be helped by the parent's attempt to present a point of view that is contrary to his real feelings on this or any other issue.

THUMB-SUCKING

Thumbsucking in a young baby should *not* be considered a bad habit that must be eliminated. It may be simply a sign that the baby is not getting enough sucking at the breast or bottle. Some authorities also see thumbsucking as a beginning of self-awareness. Sucking needs are different, in any case, from nourishment needs. Even fetuses, for example, who are, after all, "fed intravenously," have been observed to suck their thumbs. At the breast it means allowing the baby to stay on the first breast for about twenty minutes rather than removing him from the breast when he has finished taking in the milk or switching him too soon to the other breast. On the bottle it means the holes in the nipple of the bottle are too big and the baby is not getting sufficient sucking. If a bottle is used, it is highly preferable, especially during the first eight months of life, for the baby to be held by the mother, father, or parental surrogate. Thumbsucking may not only be a sign of not enough sucking, but also of not enough cuddling and holding. At this age with this in mind it obviously makes no sense to apply any sort of restraint or discouragement of thumbsucking. Your efforts should be directed toward eliminating the cause rather than dealing with the symptom.

Thumbsucking from the age of one year on represents a different situation. Now it is used as a comfort and a refuge back to an earlier period in which life had less stress or was less complicated or else was a period in which the baby got more attention and personal interaction mainly from his mother. If this occurs, it might be wise to try to figure out what may be going wrong. Is mother giving enough attention? Is she preventing the baby or child from following his interests? Is there an older child who is harassing or upsetting the baby? Is there a new baby who is taking attention away? Once the situation has been diagnosed correctly, it may be able to be remedied. Restraints such as elbow splints, bad-tasting medicines on the fingers, pulling the thumb out of the baby's mouth or bribes are not recommended or necessary up until age five. It is generally thought by most dentists that displacements of the first teeth do not have any marked influence on the regularity of second teeth. After age five when second teeth begin to come in, thumbsucking is better discouraged by rewards for *not* doing it than by punishments for doing it. It may be better still to attempt to figure out what is causing the insecurity that prompts a child to do a great deal of thumbsucking after age five. This should be done either by the parents or, if necessary, with professional help. (A later section gives advice about how to seek such professional help.)

If thumbsucking is personally offensive to *you,* however, there is no point trying to hide this from your child. What you may do is to get across to the child that this is your personal taste and that the activity itself is not necessarily bad or offensive to others. Nevertheless, you can communicate your own discomfort with it and attempt to get the child to extinguish the habit in your presence. The important issue is that you as a parent should be real. Especially after the first year or two in the child's life, you can begin to impose your will upon the child while taking the responsibility for it as your own particular idiosyncracy, avoiding moralizing or generalizing or making the child feel guilty about it. If the thumbsucking does *not* bother you, then, of course, there is no problem—at least up to age five.

EATING

Eating attitudes can have very profound effects in development, as we see. I think the general trend to follow should be to allow the child as much autonomy as possible as soon as possible. By this I mean that from *his* point of view alone, the child should decide when he will eat and what he wants to eat. Some experiments have shown that when left to their own devices, most children will automatically eat a reasonably well-balanced diet. Forcing a child to eat what is thought to be good for him usually produces all kinds of problems around eating and usually will result in his having an aversion to the very foods you are pushing. Besides the child will often experience you as being too intrusive, violating his personal boundaries. This can set up all kinds of fears of closeness in the future. Recently I appeared late at a restaurant and found that my wife had innocently and inadvertently ordered for me. I was furious at her. You can imagine how a child feels every time his mother "orders" for him or worse yet disregards his stated wishes and pushes something on him that he does not like.

Even during the first few months of life it is wise to respect a child's choices of what solid foods he eats. If he rejects a food, it may be re-introduced at a later point and over again to see whether he might have developed a liking for it. But if he consistently rejects the food, it is wise to forget about it. By about one year to eighteen months of age a child with encouragement should be feeding himself completely. Most parents worry too much about a child's nutrition. It is not a good idea to force, cajole or bribe a child to eat. Most problems that children develop in this connection grow out of a parent's well-meaning but misguided attempts to have the child eat the so-called correct foods. Actually more problems can be caused by setting up a power struggle over eating than can come from some minor nutritional lack. Severe nutritional lacks in children of middle-class American families are rare indeed.

The parent should decide at what age he wishes the child to begin to eat with him. This can vary from about age three on. Some parents actually enjoy having a three year old sitting at the table and can put up with whatever noise, spilling and other inconveniences this may involve. Other parents prefer eating in silence or by themselves and can go out of their minds even with a ten year old. Again, the parent should make the decision about this based on his own particular individuality. There is no point in a parent's having dinner with a small child and developing a hatred for the child as well as an ulcer because he absolutely cannot tolerate it but feels he must pretend it is an unmitigated joy. As soon as the child begins to eat with the family, he should be expected to eat whatever the family is eating. This does not mean that he has to eat everything on the table. However, if he clearly dislikes everything, then rather than having a special meal cooked for him, he should have the option of eating easily prepared foods such as dry cereals, fruits or sandwiches. These should be the child's responsibility to prepare, even starting at age five. Food requirements vary from child to child. If a child is especially thin or especially overweight, this represents a problem that should be presented to a pediatrician for advice.

Hours for Eating

As far as time for eating is concerned—hours, punctuality, whether or not the child should sit with parents—this would be best determined by the child's needs also *if* he were the only one involved. However, after the second year when demand feeding needs have been met, there are frequently situations in which the convenience of one or both parents makes a particular eating time for the child mandatory. Here I feel the time should be picked *for the parents' convenience* and that this should be stated openly. Children must be made to realize as quickly as possible that parents have certain privileges and powers. They have acquired these by their age and position. The home is not run as a democracy. The tone at the dinner table should also be openly set for the parents' convenience. If one or both parents cannot stand chatter at dinner, then dinner should be relatively quiet. If the parents prefer a friendly interchange, then that should be established.

Welcoming and Exclusion of Children at Family Table

Parents may choose at times or even mostly to eat separately from the children. This may especially be true if there are guests for dinner. There may be parties or other social functions when the parents' convenience would dictate that the child should not be *present.*

The child from the earliest age on should be told that there are situations in which his presence is *not* required and would cramp the parents' freedom and enjoyment.

The child can be told this openly and directly without his feeling rejected or unwanted in general. A dividing line must be made between situations in which the child is welcome and those in which he clearly is not. If the child is present at functions in which he interferes with the parents' enjoyment, this will only develop hostility in the parent toward the child which will be expressed in overt or covert ways. Besides adults are themselves constantly excluded from a variety of situations—such as meetings of the directors of a company or organization. It is unrealistic for children to grow up to expect that *they* will always be the ones who make such choices.

Along with this idea, I am reminded of comedian Sam Levenson's joke that he never had the white meat of the chicken. When he was a child, he said his parents preempted the white meat. When he became a parent, it was the fashion to give the child the best part. So, poor Sam still hasn't had the white meat! Now I am very much against this fashion of dealing with children. I think the parents should openly use their power to get their way and that even includes getting first choice of the piece of meat. I think that children who are brought up to expect that they will be favored while their parents sacrifice themselves and deprive themselves for their sake are really not being done any favors. First of all they are being presented with a totally unrealistic picture of the world. The people who have power over them in life are not going to abdicate their power and favor them. The boss is not going to come in on weekends and allow them to take time off. If anyone has a two-hour lunch period, it will be the boss—not them. To present them with the experience of being constantly favored has to be very confusing. It also presents you to them as a masochistic model. You don't want them to become self-negating martyrs. Then why should you be that way with them? Besides, by doing this kind of thing with them, you are producing feelings of guilt and obligation in them in connection with you. This will bind them to you and make it more difficult for them to separate from you. You may not consciously want to create this situation, but that is exactly what you *are* doing. Part of *letting them go* involves the knowledge of the real world your children must have if they are to be let go successfully. The authentic parent is a real person, and a real person has preferences and, with power, will exercise them—whether over life-and-death matters, or chicken breasts! I am not talking about tyranny, obviously. The division of the chicken is incidentally an interesting example of the authentic world. If everyone preferred the white meat and the chicken had only white meat, a parent might try to provide that for all. But the real facts are otherwise, and the reality is what children should be faced with.

Table Manners —Restaurants

As far as table manners go, try to get across to your children the importance (or lack of importance) of their behavior for *you*. In restaurants, the same thing applies. If you don't care how they behave, fine. If you die a thousand deaths if they talk loudly or don't observe Emily Post's etiquette, then insist on their doing it your way or don't ever take them to a restaurant. Be your authentic self. Let them know clearly how you want them to behave and that it is simply a matter of suiting you.

In general in regard to feeding, the idea is basically to be yourself, follow your own feelings, and openly acknowledge your self-interest. At the same time you should let the children have as much free choice as possible (say about choice of food) when it doesn't cramp your particular style.

Some of you who read this may recoil in horror and say, "My gosh, I did the wrong thing in every instance. I had scheduled feeding. I didn't allow enough sucking. I force-fed my child I always sacrificed what I wanted to give it to him. What can I do now?" I suppose the answer is that there is very little you can do now to change past situations that you did not handle correctly. But remember that, on the whole, human beings are very resilient, and many of us have survived and done rather well even with much worse mothering or fathering than you have given your child. If you agree with some of the theses of this book and are currently engaged in doing things that now do not make sense to you, then change them abruptly. This may be a bit confusing to your child, but he will readily accept your explanation that you have read about the issue and thought about it and have decided to handle it differently. At least that way mistakes that are currently being made will not continue. Try not to feel guilty or go into apologies to your child. These will probably create confusion and embarrassment rather than accomplishing anything positive.

"DIFFICULT" BABIES —COLIC AND OTHER PROBLEMS

Some babies are much more difficult than others. Four conditions that involve crying in the first weeks of life are called colic, periodic irritable crying, fretful baby, and hyperactive baby. Luckily they all tend to pass by the age of three months. Colic is accompanied by pain, distention and gas, and the crying is usually limited to one period in the evening or afternoon. Periodic irritable crying is the same without the gas. By a fretful baby we usually mean one who cries now and then at any time of the day or night. A hyperactive baby is very tense and irritable and has a startle reaction to sudden movements or sounds. These conditions are more a function of adjustment of the baby's nervous or digestive system than they are a function of any disturbance in the mother-child relationship. They are not at all serious and tend to pass.

It is important to relax if you possibly can about such conditions, do the best you can, and try not to feel guilty or blame yourself. You have no need to.

The mothers of these babies, however, are often quite upset and can become inordinately fatigued, physically and emotionally, from these conditions. They should certainly try to enlist the aid of their husband, mother, other relatives, or maids in sharing the care of such babies and should get away for a few hours at a time to relieve the

away to break the tension aids rather than detracts from
the overall ability to "hold them very close."

―――――――――――――HOLDING AND PHYSICAL AFFECTION

From a child's point of view the more holding and physical affection he gets the better he likes it and the better off
he is. Hold them very very close. This is especially true
during the first year of life. Here an absence of maternal
affection can bring about some emotional retardation. As
a matter of fact deprivation of holding and affection in the
first year of life—even when all other physical needs are
satisfied—can be so damaging as to result in the actual
death of the infant. During the first year of life, then, this
need is almost as strong as the need for food. From the
work that has been done in the field of child development,
I think the more holding and physical contact a baby has
the better off he is. I think the sureness of self that many
American and Central and South American Indians have
may stem from their being strapped to their mother's back
during the first and some of the second years of their lives.
This is what is good for the baby. Conversely, being left
during the first two years is experienced as a profoundly
terrifying experience by infants. However, the *quality* of
the mothering is always a factor that is more important
than the mere quantity. That is why, even if you know
that having you practically attached to your baby's skin
constantly is very good for him in general, if it drives you
out of your mind or makes you very uncomfortable, then
signals are off. The negative vibrations generated by your
anxiety or hostility will do more harm than the physical
contact does him good. But, for God's sake, if you feel
affectionate and like to hold the baby, don't inhibit yourself on the basis that it will "spoil" him. Remember, the
more affection the better. As a matter of fact all through
life all of us need to be held and cuddled. This is a need
that has to be distinguished from a sexual need. We
should get our needs for physical affection satisfied. This

can occur before sex or after sex, but it is separate from sex. And, of course, it does not have to precede or follow sex or be satisfied by an individual with whom we have a sexual relationship.

Talking about sex, one of the reasons often given for cutting down on the amount of physical contact between parents and children (especially between ages four and seven and around puberty) is that the physical affection will be too sexually stimulating to the child. I do not think this objection is generally valid. As long as the parent is not actually being sexual toward the child, I do not think the child will fail to distinguish between affection and sexuality. However if the parent is unclear about whether the contact may be sexual on his part or on the child's— say between a father and a ten-year-old daughter, caution may be wise. I think the biggest problem about sexual feelings between parents and children occurs when they are covert and expressed on either side in a hidden, guilty manner. If they are openly acknowledged—especially with humor—they are not harmful. This kind of open acknowledgment with a lightening of the situation by humor actually tends to diminish guilt and anxiety about incest taboos.

I think as far as physical affection goes—of course, providing it is genuinely felt by the parent—the more at any age the better. I also do not believe that physical affection, even that continued into adult life, retards the separation of the child from its parent. This is very important. Many other actions of parents tend to bind a child and retard separation. Physical affection does not appear to do that.

One of the most difficult distinctions for people to make is the one between behavior that binds and prevents separation and behavior that gratifies needs for love, warmth and affection. Sometimes it is difficult to tell if you are holding them close or letting them go. The distinction between these two types of behavior is confusing to many of us. A parent can be very warm, loving, and affectionate toward a child and available for physical and emotional contact without engaging in behavior that prevents the child from growing apart as much as his psychomotor development allows him. When the physical closeness or affection is needed *by* the parent *from* the child, this should be stated openly and clearly. When *I* feel a need for contact with one of my children—or from another adult for that matter—I say to them, *"I* need a hug from you." This kind of statement clearly delineates that we are separate people and that the need exists in me. If on the other hand, responding to the same need in myself, I say to the child or other person, "Come on over here. I can tell that you need a hug from me," I make a statement that prevents separation and encourages merging. It implies that you can read the other person's mind, which means that there are no boundaries between you. It also attributes to him a feeling he may not actually have. This confuses him, makes him doubt his own perceptions, implies that you know more about what he is feeling than he himself does, and damages his sense of his autonomy and separateness. Perhaps this simple example can serve as a model to distinguish between warmth and affection that can be very positive, and mind-invading behavior which can retard letting go and be very destructive.

The manner in which affection is given, then, is as important as the affection itself. If I hug my child and say, "We will always be together, I will never let you go," this is obviously more than a bestowing of spontaneous warmth. If I hug him or her and say, "I love you. You are a marvelous person," that hardly retards letting go of the child. As a matter of fact, if genuinely felt, it helps create a feeling in the child that he is a worthwhile human being and he is more likely to try to make a good emotional connection with other people without being afraid that he will be unacceptable and without putting up all kinds of defensive barriers against the fear of rejection.

It is very important for us similarly not to inhibit verbal expressions of affection such as, "You are a lovely person," "It is really a pleasure to be with you," "You are so beautiful," "You are really very bright." Parents sometimes feel they should not express such positive feelings toward children on the basis of their getting a "swelled head" or some such nonsense. Actually these expressions help a child develop a good image of himself and a feeling of confidence in his ability to be liked or loved by others. This certainly does no harm. I remember that when I described a patient of mine who was also working at a school I taught at as "a lovely person" in an evaluation, she was tremendously touched. She said neither of her parents had ever communicated anything remotely resembling this to her.

Remember, however, that if physical demonstration of affection is something that does not come naturally to you and makes you feel uncomfortable, you must always be guided by your own feelings. *Your* feelings always have the highest priority. Fake affection just confuses the child and creates many more emotional problems than no affection at all. So, as usual, who *you* are and what you feel is more important in determining what behavior of yours is best for the child than his own needs alone. This latter also applies for the time of giving affection. If a child crawls into your lap while you are eating or while you are in the process of writing this book or otherwise occupied, then it is very appropriate to refuse it at that time and to ask the child to come back later.

I do not feel that the age level has too much to do with the manner or amount of affection. Obviously infants or small children will evoke a feeling in most of us of wanting to hold them. But, if we do not screen it out as undesirable, we are likely to have this feeling toward our children even when they have become adults. There is absolutely no reason to ignore these feelings. Expressing them will be helpful and gratifying for us as well as our children. Rather than holding them too close, such expression will help let them go by giving them the feeling that others will also love them—that they are in fact lovable—and will be so even far away from you.

The most difficult and rare expressions of physical affection in our American culture are between fathers and sons. So many men grow up with an enormous unfulfilled yearning for physical affection from their fathers. Some of my most poignant moments as a therapist have been when I was able to express physical affection to a male patient.

There is a strange and very unnatural taboo in our culture against this. I would certainly encourage all fathers to express physical affection to their sons if they feel like doing so. Parenthetically, rather than encouraging homosexuality, it may be the most certain method of discouraging it. Studies on male homosexuality show that the percentage of homosexuals who received any physical affection from their fathers is infinitesimal.

But suppose—for whatever reason, perhaps even one that was unavoidable at the time—you have not expressed physical affection to your child, can you make up for it now? The answer is probably not to any major degree. Those needs are time-specific and are obviously important to the child during his first year or years of life. Being excessively affectionate at age ten is not apt to make up for what was lacking at age one, and is therefore not sensible. This is especially true, of course, if the physical affection is not natural to you and is forced, artificial, not authentically felt. If, for whatever reason, physical demonstrativeness is hard for you, then it is not wise to fake it for a child of ten. It is better to be yourself. However, genuine affection is welcome and helpful at any age (as most of us know, even as adults!). So again, as always, if you feel it, by all means express it.

———————————————————————————————SLEEPING

A very frequent question that comes up is should you go in and comfort your child when he awakes and cries. The answer is very time-specific; that is, it depends on the age of the child. Certainly purely from the child's point of view the answer during the first year would be "yes." During this time a child is quite panicky when he awakens and definitely in need of comforting.

Beginning in the second year of life, it might be wise to wait a few minutes before going in. Many times the baby will have partly but not fully awakened because of a pain, such as from teething or from a dream, but he will fall back to sleep shortly without your intervening. The first four molars come through in the average baby between the ages of a year and a year and a half and are more likely to cause trouble in sleeping than other teeth. If babies wake up and stay awake as a result of this, it might be wise to give a bit of warm milk from a cup to ease the pain. However, it is a good idea not to hold them or to extend the contact at this time, or it may lead to their maintaining the habit of waking up even after their teething is over. Holding them in the middle of the night or involving them in play or talk rewards their waking up and retards their process of separation. *You are holding them close when you should be letting them go.* The process should continue gradually through the second and third years. Obviously there may be exceptional situations such as illness or nightmares in which the quality of the cry shows that the baby is extraordinarily upset and may need special comforting. However try to make this brief as possible. Of course, children, before they have been trained, may have bowel movements or wet their diapers. These should be changed if this is the reason for their waking. Never past the first weeks should you take the child into your own room. This certainly retards the letting go process. The same thing would apply to the parent lying down with the child, especially in a regular bed. The parent will often fall asleep and end up spending the rest of the night with the child.

While I feel strongly in favor of "lying-in" or "rooming-in" arrangements directly after birth, I think it is very important once a child gets home that he have his own room if this is in any way possible economically. Despite a natural inborn tendency for all animals to snuggle and cuddle up while they sleep, I think there is a distinct disadvantage to children's sleeping in the same room as the parents or siblings. Even under very adverse circumstances, a hallway might be preferable to keeping the child in the parents' room. The rationale for not keeping the child in the parents' room even during the first year is not so much connected with the idea of holding them close or letting them go, but rather with the fact that the child will interfere with the parents' sex life. He may also be subjected to sights and sounds connected with this that are too stimulating and overwhelming to a young baby or child. In the treatment of patients in psychoanalysis one can often trace back a particular symptom or disturbing character trait to the witnessing of parental intercourse early in life. In his famous patient, "The Wolf Man," Freud was able to trace back a great deal of emotional disturbance to the man's having witnessed sex between his parents at age eighteen months. A child is apt to have severe feelings of exclusion or to experience sexuality as a hostile attack by the father upon the mother. This can lead to phobias of thunder and lightning (the symbolic representations of the sights and sounds during parental intercourse), to a tendency toward viewing sexuality in a sado-masochistic way, and to many other emotional difficulties. Now I am not implying that if your child has inadvertently had this experience once, you should reserve a room for him at the nearest psychiatric hospital. Certainly there have been many children who have had this experience and have escaped unharmed. The degree of damage done is determined by many other factors, such as how much good mothering and fathering the child has had previously and what other traumatic events may have occurred in his life. However, it is certainly wise to attempt to protect your child from this experience. Besides, from a more selfish point of view, you as a parent should not allow anything to interfere with the spontaneity and freedom of your sex life. You might very well unconsciously if not consciously resent your child's interference and take it out on him in some direct or indirect manner. I strongly recommend a lock on the parental bedroom for the sake of parents as well as children. It amazes me when I have sophisticated parents who have no lock and say they are always concerned about the children invading their room! There should be strict rules about the children's even knocking except in cases of emergency. A "Do Not Disturb" sign pilfered from a hotel can be very helpful in this regard.

I also feel it is extremely important if at all possible economically for children to have their own rooms and not be subjected to sharing rooms with siblings, grandparents, wards or other relatives. It is difficult for children, especially in their pre-teen and teen years, to share a room with a sibling of the opposite sex. It certainly increases the intensity of incestuous feelings and retards the letting go of the incestuous figure as the love object. Having a separate room is also an important part of reinforcing the child's feeling of having boundaries that are not to be invaded and of being a separate, independent, autonomous person. In this age of smaller apartments, it might be worth considering the division of one larger room into two small ones, for two children. This has been done by some parents very inexpensively. Even if the rooms are tiny, the child's pleasure in his "own" separate room can be great. This, of course, is tremendously important in aiding the process of letting the child go.

After the fourth year you should probably almost never go in when the child is crying. Continuing contact with him night as well as day would tend to reinforce his awakening and crying—by rewarding it—and would make his separation from you much more difficult. Between these two limits the answer would depend upon the specific individuality of your child as well as yourself. In terms of the former it must be remembered that all children are not alike. On one end of the spectrum there are children with some amount of brain damage who may require additional protection and firmer limits. Heredity, constitution, or previous environmental influences alone can produce very major differences between children. Even within the same family, children with essentially the same hereditary backgrounds can vary tremendously in personality.

But, of course, the other variable is you. How much do you need your sleep? How comforting can you be when you are awakened by crying? Are you so enraged at having been taken out of the arms of Morpheus that your presence induces anxiety rather than relieves it? If this is so, perhaps it is better to try to get your mate to handle this particular detail.

A short review: Pick them up at night till they're about a year; till two wait a bit; by four, don't go in at all except in emergencies.

Another frequent question is about when to set bedtime for children. Up until the age of about twelve most children do not show good enough judgment to be able to set a time for their going to bed. Requirements for sleep do vary from child to child. Children, however, may not choose of their own accord to get as much sleep as they need if they are upset, angry, over-stimulated by television, anxious, or lonely. You as the parent, therefore, will have to set up a schedule of how much sleep they should have, and you should adhere to it firmly. A very general rule of thumb is that infants usually take as much sleep as they need. From two years of age on you cannot leave it up to the child. Two year olds generally require twelve hours of sleep at night and usually a nap of an hour or so during the day. Even if the child does not sleep, the nap can constitute a time of rest—for both parent and child— and should continue up until age five. Up to age six, the child should have about twelve hours of sleep at night. From then up until about age twelve this can be diminished by about yearly one-half-hour intervals. After age twelve most children use enough good judgment to be able to determine their own sleep requirements. This is especially true if their parents give them the freedom to do so. If the parents are rigid about sleep time after age twelve, the children may use sleeping less time than they need as a way of expressing rebellion against parents. From the point of view of the child's own good alone, he should probably be given as much autonomy and flexibility as possible. But this is not the only consideration. Your need to have your privacy without the children up and around is also a prime consideration. And, since this is so, you might well be better off and they as well if you sent them to their room not for *their* own good or *their* need for sleep, but because of your own needs, which you can admit freely to them. They will respect your right to decide for them on the basis of your self-interest as long as you don't try to deceive them as to what your real reason is. If you tell them they must go to bed because they are sleepy, and they know in fact that they are not, you will only confuse them.

This is another example of how the handling of a situation can either promote separateness and individuation in a child or retard it. It is another important example of the "letting them go" process. If you state that you are sending them to their room because of your own needs for privacy, you are clearly distinguishing between yourself and them, your needs and their needs. If on the other hand you use the mind-invading tactic of sending them off because *they* are sleepy and they need to get sleep, you are not only being dishonest, but you are dissolving the boundaries between yourself and your child. You are claiming that *you* know how he feels and what he needs better than he does. You are pretending to be able to be inside of him. If he believes you, you have clouded his view of himself as a separate, autonomous person. You are not being real, and you are promoting his doubt of his own feelings and his impression that you have some omniscient connection to him. Mild mistakes along these lines may not prove too costly, but children whose parents consistently tell them what they are feeling and thinking can be tremendously destructive to the children's sense of themselves as individuals.

REWARD AND PUNISHMENT

It might be wise at this juncture to go into the whole concept of reward and punishment. In psychology there is a total theoretical approach to understanding people that is called Learning Theory. To make it very simple—too simple, I'm sure—it states that people learn through reward and punishment. If something they do is rewarded, they tend to keep on doing it. If something they do is punished, they stop doing it. Some of you will remember reading about Pavlov's experiments with dogs along these lines. The recent increase in the use of Behavior Modification Therapy is an example of a very sophisticated refinement of this theoretical approach. Even psychologists who differ tremendously with learning theory as a basic theoretical model for human behavior all accept its basic tenets and its universal application. For instance, psychoanalysts, who perhaps use learning theory least in their work, still all agree to its basic validity. Every parent should understand the fundamentals of learning theory and never forget them while he or she is bringing up a child. We constantly must reinforce behavior we want to continue with rewards. Conversely we must attempt to extinguish undesirable behavior with punishments. When a child has a temper tantrum and we accede to his wishes, we are reinforcing his temper tantrums. Any child who continually repeats some behavior that is undesirable must be getting something out of it. If every time a child whimpers at night we go in and comfort him, he will continue to whimper. If he hits us and we laugh and say how cute he is, he will continue to hit us. If he consistently comes late for dinner and we do not punish him in some way, he will continue to do so. Many parents, it seems to me, completely forget the basic tenets of learning theory in bringing up their children. They seem to forget the idea of rewarding desirable behavior as well as its opposite. When a child does something especially well or behaves in a manner that is especially pleasing to you, be sure to communicate your pleasure and your appreciation to her with words, a hug, a kiss, a goody or some extra privilege. When he does something that in your point of view is undesirable, say something to him, show your displeasure and, if appropriate, deprive him of some privilege. Keeping learning theory in mind constantly would almost by itself produce a tremendous revolution in making your child into the kind of person you want him to be.

TOILET TRAINING: "THE BATTLE OF THE CHAMBER POT"

Toilet training is one subject on which the previous books have really proved to be correct. When toilet training is instituted too early or accomplished in too harsh a manner, it can result in some very severe personality problems and psychosomatic disorders. It can cause a person to become very compulsive or be swamped with obsessive thoughts. It can generate a great deal of rage, resulting in a compulsively rebellious or even sadistic personality. It can bring about a great many sexual disorders and also spastic colitis, constipation, diarrhea, ulcerative colitis, hemorrhoids, and other anal problems. So, it might really pay off to try to stretch your own personal inclinations to their absolute limits in this particular area. Up until about age three the longer you postpone the training and the gentler you can be and the less of a power struggle you create with your child in the process, the better it will turn out ultimately for your child.

Actually children who were brought up in this manner have proven to be less driven and compulsive than those who were trained early and in a rigid way. With some individual variation it may be a good idea around age two to have a potty around and available and gently encourage its use, being very willing to back off if the child does not accept it.

It is especially important to use as many rewards for good performance as possible, and, in contrast to some other aspects of child-rearing, it is better *not* to use punishment. If you can manage not to show or express disgust with bowel or bladder functions, it will also be very helpful. I have a great many patients whose problems often stem at least in part from their parents having evinced disgust at their toilet functions. They sometimes have grown up with the feeling that they are disgusting, dirty, offensive people who will be found utterly loathsome by others. When this image of themselves and their bodies is subjected to psychoanalytic scrutiny, it boils down to the fact that what is so terrible about them is that they defecate and urinate. Unconsciously they feel they are the only ones in the world who do this and that everyone else is clean and pure. When the root of this attitude is traced back, it invariably is a reflection of their parents' attitude toward their excretory functions.

The "battle of the chamber pot" and its outcome is one of the major contributions of classical psychoanalytic theory. Up until the point of toilet training the child has things pretty much his way. His parents have hopefully tried in the main to gratify his instinctual urges rather than thwart them or contain them or control them. The onset of toilet training marks the end of this Garden of Eden and one of the first confrontations with a world that places its own demands upon the child—demands that emanate from the civilization in that world and not from anything inside the child. Pursuing an analogy from the animal kingdom we must realize that there is nothing essentially unnatural about urinating and defecating at will, enjoying the process and finding the excreted material interesting and fascinating (e.g. dogs sniffing other dogs' excretion). Toilet training, though obviously necessary for our particular type of civilization, tends to go *against* nature rather than with it. And it tends to change a fascination with excrement to a disgust with it. Such a basic change of attitude, as well as behavioral changes that are elicited, cannot be accomplished with ease or without a certain degree of strife.

In our culture the mother is almost always the major figure involved in toilet training, so I shall refer to her. I have run into only two people who were toilet trained by men. Some of my patients were toilet trained by maids. I, strangely enough, was toilet trained by my grandfather, due to rather unusual circumstances, and one of my female patients was trained by her father. For myself, I do not feel that the sex of the person was particularly significant. For my female patient the experience reinforced a very strong and erotically tinged relationship to her father. I will refer to the parent figure as the mother for the sake of convenience. I strongly applaud feminist ideas that stress the advantages of both parents being involved as equally as is feasible in child rearing.

When the mother begins toilet training too early or too strictly, it creates an important conflict for the child. I have seen patients who were trained before the age of one year, when they barely had the neurological development (and certainly not the psychological development) to institute sphincter control. The development of their character showed the effect of this trauma. The child is faced with the Hobson's choice of either subverting his own self, his will and his autonomy and becoming a subservient or compliant person *or* attempting to maintain himself and his identity and engaging in a sado-masochistic struggle with his mother that may lead the way to his having a great deal of strife with authority and perhaps an angry, volatile relationship with the person closest to him later in life. Eric Berne's parent-child-adult formulation is especially helpful in understanding some of the possible eventualities of this struggle. Instead of developing into an ideal adult who never does anything he disapproves of, is therefore never guilty or self-critical and, on the other hand, never refrains from doing anything he wishes to do since there is a balance between his desires and his conscience, the person grows up in conflict. He carries in himself the child and the parent of the "battle of the chamber pot" rather than the adult. His inner parent can be a very rigid one who inhibits naturalness, and his child may be a very compliant, good little boy or "Miss Goody Two-Shoes." This will make him prim and proper and judgmental of others in a disapproving way and at the same time compliant and inhibited. It is important that because of the anatomical contiguity of the sexual and excretory systems, problems around the anal and urinary areas are frequently transposed to the sexual area as well. General compliance to authority and inability to assert oneself are often accompanied by inhibitions in the sexual area as well. Or, conversely, the inner pattern may take the form of a rebellious child and an angry or sadistic parent. Here we end up with a person who may be always in trouble with the established order—often much to his own detriment—and simultaneously very angry and even sadistic toward people who do not do things *his* way.

Another aspect of the "battle of the chamber pot" concerns attitudes toward giving and withholding. That is one of the original issues between parent and child. The parent wants the child to give excrement at her discretion, not the child's. The child can either comply or withhold or lose control and release at will. Attitudes toward money —being very cheap or extravagant—toward collecting or disposing of items—being a compulsive collector—toward giving of time, feelings, or objects either too much or too little also are affected by the outcome of this battle or lack of battle.

I have gone into some of the far-reaching results of this battle because I want to impress you with the importance of avoiding it as much as possible and not making it into a war. Also, as some of you may have guessed, my grandfather did not handle it too gently or too well. What is perhaps even worse than being overly authoritarian and rigid is being inconsistent in this respect—a parent who is totally rigid one day and then almost encourages rebellion the next. I have seen patients who had this kind of parent. The results are really disastrous and produce total confusion, as we might imagine.

From the point of view of letting go of a child, one of the greatest boons you can give him is to respect his autonomy and not push him to perform for you on the potty until he is neurologically and psychologically ready to do so. The manner in which this is handled by the parent has a major impact on the child's sense of self and his expectation that he will be able to assert himself effectively with other people without being overly compliant or overly rebellious.

Now suppose you have just finished reading this section and you realize that you have handled the whole toilet training incorrectly. You started it too soon; you were rigid and unyielding; you used punishment instead of reward, and so on. What can you do now? Well, if the training has already been accomplished, there is very little that you can do to reverse the effects. Try to remember that you did the best you knew how and that people have survived much worse traumata than that without any very very severe results. Don't feel guilty and try not to repeat the mistakes with the next child, if there is one. One might ask, "Should I try to undo it by being very permissive or overpermissive for the rest of his childhood?" The answer to that is definitely "no." Being permissive during toilet training is good, but being permissive later is often detrimental, as we shall see. Trying to even it out by being permissive later just compounds the problem. If you are in the middle of toilet training and agree with my ideas and feel comfortable in doing things that way without losing your authenticity, then change in midstream. It may be a bit confusing to your child at first, as I've said earlier, but it will pay off in the long run.

A special mention should be made in this section about the use of enemas. I have seen several female patients many of whose problems were seriously compounded by their parents' repeated use of enemas during their childhood. The experience of being held down and having a tube inserted in the anus and then feeling the pain as the water enters the rectum is very frequently sexualized as a kind of masochistic rape experience by women. As a matter of fact a goodly number of women have sexual fantasies that revolve around being given an enema. The proximity of the anus and the vagina encourages this. Repeated forced enemas certainly can create a climate which may later lead to viewing intercourse as a masochistic experience. So frequently do repeated enemas lead to sexual and psychological distortions that they should be avoided except in cases of dire emergency and at the behest of a pediatrician who says they are absolutely vital.

CLEANLINESS AND ORDERLINESS

A great many issues that arise out of toilet training also apply to the parents' treatment of cleanliness and orderliness in a child. However, there are several important age-specific factors. What makes good sense at age two may not apply at all at age six or nine. How to handle a nine year old whose room is a mess involves a great many issues different from how to deal with putting a two year old on the potty. Whereas it is crucial in the two year old to try to bend as much as possible to his emotional needs, with the older child after toilet training has been accomplished, the reverse is almost true. First of all *you* have to decide where you stand about cleanliness and orderliness. If the lack of it does not disturb you in the least, then as in most situations it is best to let the child make as many decisions and have as many choices as possible. If on the other hand you are very upset by a lack of order or personal cleanliness in your child, then openly enforce your way of doing things on him. Again do not rationalize that you are doing this because "cleanliness is next to Godliness" or it is more *moral* or righteous to be clean. Make it clear that this is your personal preference or even idiosyncracy, that you want things your way, that you have the power in the house, and that you will impose your will for this reason. Make it clear that when the children grow up and are out of your sphere of influence, they can choose some other way to go about things. I have seen many parents in constant arguments with their children about their rooms being a mess. This is because they vacillate in expressing clearly their point of view and their power to enforce it, for instance by withholding allowances and restricting their privileges. Some people may say, "Doesn't the child have the right to keep his room his way as long as the door is closed?" The answer is "Yes, absolutely," but *not* if what goes on behind that closed door drives you up a wall because of your own compulsiveness. If you try to let them keep their own room their way because of some belief in "children's rights," but in truth the disorder annoys you and creates a great deal of resentment in you, you will ultimately take it out on your children to their detriment. A forced and faked attitude of permissiveness on your part will only produce confusion in them and will probably encourage a continual battle that may be displaced to another arena, such as getting angry when they break a dish. Even if your attitude appears totally neurotic and reprehensible to most people, it is better for your child to have this attitude expressed "up front" rather than having it leak out and sneak out in covert ways that are much more apt to engender neurotic problems in the child. A child can separate out from and rebel against your imperfections and irrationalities as long as you don't pretend not to have them. The falseness and sham of pretending to be a perfect, kind, totally understanding individual as a parent is much more destructive than even overt destructiveness. The idea is to be *real*, not to pretend to be some ideal parental archetype. Be authentic rather than the way you think you are supposed to be. Don't pull yourself out of shape because you want the kids to like you. Don't worry about their *liking* you. Do what's best for you. That is ultimately what is best for them because it will aid your letting go of them by showing them that they are different and separate from you.

The same ideas apply to taking baths, brushing teeth, washing hair, washing hands after going to the toilet, and so on. Actually none of these, with the exception of brushing teeth, have much effect on general health and certainly no connection with morality. Children should be told that they must wipe themselves after defecating and girls after urinating to prevent local infections. Sometimes children in pre-teen and teen years, especially if their parents have been compulsive, will drive them crazy by spending what seems like hours in the bathroom. Here it may be well to remember that you are now sowing what you have reaped. It seems particularly unfair to be terribly compulsive about cleanliness when a child is young and then to chastise him for being compulsive in his later years.

One of the special blights of teen-age years is acne. As a sufferer from this myself during those years, I have a particular sympathy for children who have the misfortune to go through it. I include it under this heading because from a subjective point of view a child feels dirty and disgusting and totally unacceptable when he or she has this skin disease. I can only recommend most highly a sympathetic and empathetic understanding of the child's reaction to it. In talking about empathy, it is important to distinguish between empathy and reassurance. If you tell a child who has acne that he is still beautiful and acceptable, it will make very little impression on him. If you tell him you understand how badly he feels and how unacceptable he experiences himself to be, this is infinitely more helpful. I remember one occasion when I was feeling totally down, depressed and despairing. I remember my wife telling me that I had nothing to feel badly about, that the situation was not really serious, that I had so many things to feel good and happy about. This went on for hours, and I sank further and further into despair. Finally after about five hours she said, "Oh, I understand. You really feel lousy." I heaved a sigh of relief and immediately felt better. At last there was someone who could understand what I was experiencing. This might be a good thing to keep in mind when a child or for that matter an adult is feeling badly. Nostrums or words of encouragement are often the worst possible response.

So, coming back to the acne, it is very important to take your teen-ager's reaction to it seriously and to try to be as helpful as it is natural for you to be in advising creams, diets, and if necessary, dermatologists. Aside from acne, pre-teen and teen-agers are often very sensitive to other real or imagined imperfections in their appearance—such as moles, small or large breasts, ungainly ears or noses. There is a special focus on such defects at this age level. This is tied in with the child's body image and reflects his having a poor sense of his appearance, a negative self-image. It does little good to reassure a child at this age that he or she is really beautiful. *Empathy is more effective than reassurance.*

When the issue becomes monumentally important psychically and there is a real anatomical defect in ears or nose, for example, that can rather safely and easily be corrected by plastic surgery, this approach should not be ruled out, though of course it must be thought about in psychological as well as cosmetic terms. Rarely will it solve the problem, but in a few rare instances it can be extremely helpful.

SEX

This is another subject on which ideas that were promulgated by parent education books tended to be very helpful and prove to have been correct. I think there is no doubt that children who were brought up by "enlightened" parents have significantly fewer sexual problems and sexual anxieties than their parents did. From the point of view of the child alone, without consideration at this point of the parents' personality, I feel that the more permissive parents can be about sex, the less apt the child is to have difficulties in this area. I would actually go beyond being permissive. If you yourself can feel comfortable enough not only to permit but to encourage sexual activity such as masturbation in your children, it would be good for them. In my view masturbation should not only be tolerated, it should be openly encouraged. Masturbation is not only the beginning of the enjoyment of sexual pleasure; it is also a very important cornerstone in the development of a sense of self. Like thumbsucking, it is one of the first ways we have of knowing that we can derive pleasure by ourselves from our own bodies. It is also one of the important steps in the development of a healthy narcissism or love of our own bodies and encourages in us a positive image of our own bodies.

Many of us unfortunately will feel much too uncomfortable to encourage masturbation. It was one of the strongest taboos in former generations. In my book, *Sexual Fulfillment and Self-Affirmation,* I suggest that one of the greatest things that could happen in America would be to have a monument in honor of masturbation erected in Times Square. It is a bit too much, however, to ask of ourselves as parents to go from seeing masturbation as one of the greatest sins and taboos to being able to encourage it openly in our children. But again from their point of view alone, this might be for the ultimate good. The only restriction that should be imposed upon masturbation, of course, is the appropriateness of the place in which it is performed. It makes no sense to me to visit a friend and see a child masturbating openly in the middle of the living room. Even if this does not offend the parents, it may certainly offend the guests.

EDUCA-TION AND ATTITUDES The best way to handle children's questions about sex is to answer as fully and as frankly as befits the child's ability to understand within the limits of your own knowledge of the answer. If you don't know, it's better to say that you don't know. If you can manage it, it is better to use explicit anatomical and medical terms when talking about sex rather than euphemisms. The avoidance of directness has to suggest to the child that there is something secret and forbidden about sex.

There is currently a controversy about whether sex is a subject that should be taught at school or handled exclusively by parents. My own feeling is very much in favor of sex education in schools because I feel that if it is treated like any other subject in which the dissemination of knowledge is advantageous, it becomes a less secret, forbidden, compartmentalized part of life. Now I am sure that some readers will feel strongly in the opposite direction—that sex information should be given exclusively by parents because they feel it involves delicate and controversial issues. Such parents should certainly do what they can to keep sex education out of the schools their children attend (or keep their children out of schools in which it is taught). Again, of course, the point is for you as a parent to be authentic.

Menstruation, intercourse, ejaculations, homosexuality, and other issues should all be explained to a child *whenever he begins to ask about them or by age ten, if he has not asked specifically.* Certainly a girl should understand all about menstruation before her first period occurs. If not, as happened to many of my patients, she will be shocked and dismayed. If you cannot handle informing them for any reason, then let someone you trust to be clear, mature, and explicit do it for you. I think it is part of the parents' responsibility to give birth-control information to their children or at least to recommend them to a person who can dispense the information clearly and accurately. Giving knowledge about birth control does not necessarily mean advocating its use. All forms of sex education are education rather than license.

Now with all of this about what attitudes are ideal for bringing up a child without sexual inhibitions or problems, you must remember that *you* are still the responsible parent. If it makes you uncomfortable to talk to your children about sex or even to hear them talk about sex in your presence, then it is better to acknowledge this as a personal idiosyncracy or even limitation. But, if you have strong religious, moral, or personal views about sex and a great deal of conviction about them, then it is important for you to impart them and to impose them. You must first and foremost be true to yourself. You should not pretend to espouse points of view that are basically alien to you because they are "good" for your child. The process of your talking out of both sides of your mouth simultaneously or else talking one way and acting another way would merely set up a confusion in the child's mind. I also think this applies to parents who may have different and conflicting views about sex. I do not believe that "parents should present a united front" on this or any other issue. A united front is a *front*—not an honest expression of individual feelings. I had the experience myself of holding and imparting views very divergent from my wife's about sexual freedom to our teen-age daughter. She ultimately had to make up her own mind.

NUDITY   Nudity is also very much a matter of personal parental choice. Being natural and being oneself is the key. Certainly there is nothing essentially harmful about nudity. If a parent has no inhibitions about it, he will neither go out of his way to expose himself, nor will he run to hide himself. However, if he feels very embarrassed about being exposed, he will be better off and so will his child if he consistently covers himself than if he does not and shows all kinds of anxiety and embarrassment.

Certainly if a parent exposes himself or herself to a child as a way of being seductive rather than in the natural course of events, this can result in the child's being bound to the parent through sex. It will make it more difficult for the child to let go of the parent and find a non-incestuous love object. If you have any doubts about your own conscious or unconscious motivation in exposing yourself to your child, perhaps it would be safer to forgo it. A seductive kind of exposure can be harmful whereas less harm is likely to result from avoiding any exposure. Nudity among siblings is almost impossible to avoid and is not

harmful. During pre-teen and teen years a natural degree
of modesty usually sets in to exert a built-in control.

Parents and children do have sexual feelings about one **SEXUAL**
another. If this can be accepted as natural and even han- **FEELINGS**
dled with a sense of humor, it should not cause any great **BETWEEN**
difficulties. The Oedipus complex and the incest taboo, **PARENTS**
while probably having some innate biological as well as **AND**
cultural roots, seemed a more important psychological is- **CHILDREN**
sue in other cultures and in the past than it is in present-
day America. As a matter of fact, the discoveries about the
Oedipus complex and the dissemination of psychoanalytic insights about incest are probably the reasons
why incestuous thoughts or feelings ceased in our society
to represent the horror that they formerly did. But many
of us parents are not so liberated as to be able to tolerate
such ideas easily.

The idea of its being not unnatural for children to have
sexual feelings toward us and conversely for us to have
these feelings toward them (*not* to act them out), even if
it is accepted intellectually by many of us, may still be
rather threatening emotionally. Some of us may not be
casual enough about such feelings either to discuss them
openly with our children or to be able to joke about them.
I am sure most parents deal with this issue by avoiding it
completely. While this may not be the absolutely optimal
way to handle the feelings, it does not cause any undue
harm either.

A question that comes up in connection with this issue is **SEX PLAY**
how to handle sex play among siblings. Such play is **AMONG**
hardly unusual or unlikely. Heterosexual activity may **SIBLINGS**
well occur when one of the children is in the four to seven
range or the pubertal age. Homosexual sex play for either
sisters or brothers is more common between the ages of
eight and the onset of puberty. Most parents will not be
able to tolerate it to any degree and will put a stop to it

if they become aware of it. This is certainly in line with being an authentic parent. Most of us parents have been brought up with very strong taboos against incest. The discouragement of sexual activity between siblings, especially if it is done without too much shame or humiliation, is probably the best most of us can do. There is certainly no harm in this, and it may help push the child toward a non-incestuous choice of love object. The only time it is really terribly essential to stop this behavior, however, is if there is a marked age differential between the children and the older one is exposing the younger one to stimuli that he or she cannot handle emotionally.

In the past psychoanalytic circles stressed the tremendously damaging effects of incestuous sex in childhood with either parents or older siblings. I have had the opportunity to treat in depth several patients who have had such experiences. I have been rather surprised in general to discover in these patients an absence of extremely severe repercussions in later life and even in sexual adjustment. That is not to say that I would advocate such experiences or encourage them by any means. However, the patients who have had these experiences did not appear any more devastated by them than other patients were by other kinds of experiences. I recall especially a young woman patient who had extensive and continuing incestuous sexual experiences from age eleven right through her teen years. She had an excellent sexual adjustment and although she did have some psychological problems, they were no more than most patients'. So my answer to what to do about sex between siblings would be: stop it without shaming or humiliating the children. This would be your authentic emotional response to it and probably the most helpful to the child.

TEEN-AGE SEX How a parent should handle a teen-ager's increasing interest in sex is a very personal decision based on your own cultural, religious, and even philosophical views about life. Being very permissive and even encouraging about sexual contacts and expressions may very well result in your child being free and uninhibited about sex. However, this may be quite the opposite of your conscious goal for him. You may want a child who never has any premarital or extramarital sexual experience. How you handle his coming home with *Playboy* or Henry Miller may vary considerably according to your beliefs. My own personal and professional experience has been that children brought up in an atmosphere of complete sexual freedom do not run toward sexual excesses nor are they overly preoccupied with sexual experience. Rather they tend to take sex as a matter of course and to give it an appropriate weight in their list of priorities. I would also acknowledge that they are more likely than not to want a number and variety of premarital and perhaps extramarital sexual experiences. If this appears from your vantage point to be totally or in the main extremely undesirable, then permissiveness along sexual lines will probably not suit you.

It has been traditional in our culture to be permissive to male children, encouraging them to have many sexual experiences, while encouraging chastity and virginity in female children. To some, especially feminists, like myself, this may seem patently unfair. However, others with a more traditional view of male-female relationships and differences may find this idea to their liking.

DATING

There is such a personal and individual variation in the age at which sexual experiences begin that statistics are of little help in determining your attitudes about when to allow your children to start dating (usually from twelve or thirteen on), when to stop setting specific curfews (usually about sixteen or seventeen), and how to handle the introduction of specifically erotic material into the house by your children. Needless to say, the clearer you are about your own attitudes toward these issues, and the more forcefully you transmit them, the better it is for the child. Part of letting him go is to present your own views and beliefs as directly as possible. Then he will have a base against which to separate out his own views, perhaps in agreement, perhaps in disagreement with yours. Even a position of total sexual freedom should not be presented as "Anything you do is OK." Rather you should present your own views and your rationale for having them. Sexual permissiveness should not be seen as an abdication of parental authority but as a very forthright point of view that is promulgated with as much zeal as sexual restrictions are. If you present yourself clearly to your child, whatever your point of view is, he will know where you stand and will have a base from which to launch his own separate position—either one like yours or one quite different from it.

DISCIPLINE

To quote Dr. Benjamin Spock (*Redbook,* February 1974), "Inability to be firm is, to my mind, the commonest problem of parents in America today." He goes on to blame professionals in the field for undermining the self-assurance of parents. (Dr. Spock has written on this at greater length in a book called *Raising Children in a Difficult Time.*) I do agree that this was an unfortunate result of the series of books on how to be a good parent. Parents were torn between their intuition, the use of their own parents as role-models, and the books that told them what they should do, which created a stereotype for them. The result was often a complete confusion in their minds. Sometimes they would be one way, sometimes another, and often they would "solve" the problem by completely abdicating their parental roles, providing no firm guidelines for the children to follow. There is really only one way for a parent to act that will have any consistency, and that is for him to be himself.

Discipline during the first year of a child's life does not make much sense and will not produce much of an effect. When the child starts walking at the beginning of the first year, physical restraints such as playpens and walkers are sometimes helpful as long as they are not overused. Rather than being restrictive, they protect the child from unnecessary physical trauma and relieve the mother's anxiety. After that each parent has to decide where *he* stands on how much discipline or lack of it makes him comfortable. Within his own self-determined limits, each parent should run a tight ship. He should decide which issues are important to him and impose his views without being apologetic and with as little vacillation as possible.

Transgressions against one parent should be handled by *that* parent, not turned over to the other for punishment.

A solid framework or structure is important for a child. It is more important to *have* a stable structure than to have any particular structure. Inconsistency in parental discipline and abdication of the parents' leadership role is more harmful than the imposition of an unjust order, whatever that may be defined to be. The parent should insist on respect for his position. He has the physical, financial and intellectual power, and he should use it to impose his will in his own particular style. Misguided concepts of "fairness" have crippled parents and ultimately their children.

Physical punishment will rarely if ever be required if the proper attitude is adopted. The problem with physical punishment is usually not the physical damage or pain it inflicts, but rather the humiliation that it produces in a child. Some of the most difficult analytic patients I have treated are those who have had severe problems with humiliation. Their oversensitivity to this emotion causes them tremendous hurt and often brings about major difficulties in relating to others. If a parent can express himself honestly to a child through words, there should rarely if ever be a need for physical punishment. Even if you have been brought up to hit children, you should try your utmost not to express yourself in this way. The only example to the contrary might be a gentle slap on the behind to teach a child to avoid danger, such as crossing a street against the light.

I want to elaborate on some of the enormous psychic damage done to children through beating. I have been treating a young woman who was beaten very severely by her father right up until she was age twenty-three. The girl's mother would report any misconduct to him, and he would beat the girl. During the course of the beatings the father would lose control completely, swing wildly and beat her so severely that the mother would have to intervene literally to save her life. These beatings were administered all through her life on the average of two or three times a month. During these beatings the girl would not cry and would continue to be defiant. She felt that the only way she could preserve her pride was not to capitulate totally by dissolving into tears. Her humiliation from these beatings was so painful to her—even more than the physical pain, which was severe enough—that to capitulate by crying would have left her feeling totally destroyed as a person.

What this girl and then young woman did in reaction to these experiences was to develop a very tough façade. She became *like* her father and would frequently verbally humiliate her close friends, her lovers, and then her husband. One can imagine the severe interpersonal difficulties this caused her. Even while maintaining this protective façade, she remained terribly sensitive to the slightest real or imagined "put-down" by anyone including me, her analyst. It was only after many years of analysis that she was able to relinquish her characterological defenses and become involved in a relationship in which she allowed more vulnerability and closeness and was less defended.

Of course humiliation does not arise only from physical punishment, though it does almost invariably accompany it. Other forms of punishment may also carry strong elements of humiliation. I had a patient whose mother would hang out his soiled diapers in the window so everyone in the small town in which he lived could ridicule him. Punishment in front of peers, contemporaries, or siblings is often accompanied by strong feelings of humiliation. The way some parents address their children or scream at them robs them of all dignity and respect. Punishment should merely have as its goal the extinction of undesirable (to that particular parent) behavior. It should not seek to destroy the child's self-image or his pride or to produce shame or humiliation. With this in mind it seems to me the best kinds of punishments are those that withhold privileges, such as allowances, sleep-overs, watching TV, going to the movies, sweets, and the like. These punishments hit the mark without harming the child's ego. Punishment should obviously not interfere with the parents' freedom. If you punish a small child by not allowing him to go out and play, remember that you may be punishing yourself more by having him inside the house all day! In my twenty-fifth anniversary college report, one of my classmates said, "I thought that things were tough on Guadalcanal. But I had no idea what hell was really like till I spent a rainy weekend at home with my five children." It is not a good idea to punish children by sending them to their room. Their room for them should be hallowed ground, their own turf, a place that establishes boundaries for them from the rest of the world. Using the room for banishment, as a dungeon or jail, interferes with this concept.

A form of behavior that should be avoided because it humiliates children is talking about them in their presence, especially negatively. To talk about them, yet not to them, is dehumanizing and degrading. Adults usually try not to talk in the third person about other adults in their presence; it is equally unpleasant and punitive in front of children. There is nothing inherently authentic about plain rudeness!

Another form of punishment—not talking to the child at all, thereby withholding communication—is also not advisable and is really "dirty pool," since it threatens the child's relationship with you, rather than merely trying to modify the nature of the relationship. Sarcasm, teasing, and nagging are also poor forms of punishment because they always involve a degree of humiliation. The same would apply to yelling and screaming at a child. Some recent studies have shown that children would rather be hit than yelled at. I do not believe in hitting children, but I must say that I remember myself at the age of five when my father was yelling at me interminably, saying to him, "Why don't you get a hairbrush and spank me with it like other fathers do, instead of yelling at me so long?" The yelling was clearly more humiliating to me than I imagined the spanking would be. I recall that in fact he took my advice, gave me a few perfunctory strokes and stopped yelling. The hitting—at least in response to *my* request—had less humiliation connected with it.

It is very important to stick to whatever rule you impose. If you say your child must be home at seven, then you must punish him in some significant way if gets home at seven ten. Otherwise he will not follow you the next time you impose a rule. Impose as few or as many rules as you wish and as suit your particular personality and values. But once you have imposed a rule, stand by it. If you don't, your child will very correctly assume that your rules do not need to be followed. Then one day he will break one and you will be furious, but he will not be able to comprehend why you are angry. Rules are like maps or guides. They make us feel secure and give us an external structure in which to operate. Most adults cannot handle total freedom. Children certainly cannot. Erich Fromm, the psychologist, wrote a famous book, *Escape from Freedom,* that describes the anxiety that freedom generates even in adults.

FREEDOM AND EDUCATION

With this in mind I might make a slight detour off the established course of this book to make a few personal comments on my views on progressive education and the trend toward "open classrooms," "alternative high schools," and the like. I remember on my first day of college the Dean of Freshmen addressed us, saying, "What you get out of college will depend on what you put into it. Of course, those of you who come from progressive schools will learn how to read and write." The idea of teaching children and growing adults by diminishing outside structure and controls and allowing them to follow their own inclinations, though it may sound marvelous in theory, does not seem to work in fact. If most adults cannot handle freedom, how can children and adolescents manage it when they are involved in a learning process much of which is admittedly dull and boring and must be

accomplished through rote memory? I went to an extraordinarily difficult and structured high school that made
tremendous demands on me. I often say that I have been
coasting ever since on what I learned in my time there.
From there I entered Harvard College with what was supposed to be the most elite group of bright, intellectual, and
creative young men. At Harvard we were treated as mature adults. There was no attendance taken and no com-
pulsion to attend classes. We were supposed to be so
mature that the way we apportioned our time was left to
us. Our only responsibility was to pass the examinations
at the end of the semester. Almost all of my friends and
myself (theretofore a very diligent student) responded to
this trust by taking every "snap" course that was offered,
going to class only when absolutely necessary, and pass-
ing the examinations by cheating or using other students'
notes. I became a rather good contract bridge player during my years there and developed several close and valuable friendships, but that was the extent of my edification.
My thought is that, if that was the fate of an elite group
of Harvard students, I can imagine what must be happening to more ordinary students in grade school or junior
high school or high school across the country as well
as to college students. My own experience with the new
forms of education is that, with a few exceptions,
the results are often disastrous. Children need a clear
structure in which to operate. The very existence of this
structure allows them to separate from it in their own
individual, autonomous way. The lack of structure impedes self-actualization; it does not promote it as the
theorists would have us believe. Structure helps us to let
go of children and helps them to let go of us.

There may be some exceptionally mature children or
adolescents who really can flourish best in an atmosphere
of permissiveness, but these appear to me to be in the
small minority. This kind of education puts tremendous
demands on the teacher, and few teachers, save those
extremely gifted, will be able to pull off this miracle.

A friend of mine married a woman with three children
from a previous marriage. She was vacillating in her disci-

pline, going from total permissiveness to violent physical outbursts. Her ex-husband had totally abdicated his role. Her twelve-year-old son had already had two scrapes with the police for violating minor rules about where to ride his bicycle, and he was having problems with his teachers. Her ten-year-old daughter was a constant complainer, and the younger daughter had temper tantrums. My friend came into the family and immediately took over with very explicit rules about what could and could not be done, what would and would not be tolerated. At first, the children broke all the rules and made fun of his authoritarian stance. But every time they broke a rule, he firmly punished them by withholding their allowances or not permitting some particular privilege. Within a few months all of the son's scrapes with the police and teachers had stopped, and so had the middle child's complaining and the younger one's tantrums. Instead of hating him, they all got along very well with him and developed a close, affectionate relationship with him.

This approach is in marked contrast with our so-called Spocked children. In these "Spocked" instances, as I have said before, the parent did not set enough guidelines and the child was led to believe that he could draw his own blueprint. He also became imbued with the idea that whatever he did or did not do was exactly the way his parents wanted him to behave. There was a total blurring of boundaries between parent and child so that the child never effected a real emotional separation from the parent. He often had no idea how the parent really felt about him or his behavior. The blank check of complete positive acceptance turned out to be counterfeit. The complete acceptance was like no real acceptance at all, no real concern, and only an abdication of parental responsibility. Without the clear emotional concept of the parent, the child could not establish a turf of his own on which to make individual stands and choices and have value systems that he could see as different from his parents' and autonomous for himself. Instead of the parents' letting go of the child through this non-interference, they unwittingly bound the child to themselves by creating a con-

fused person involved in a murky merger with an unclear
parental image.

Being a firm disciplinarian once you have determined the structure that suits you is not being mean or inconsiderate. In fact, not being one shows a real lack of responsibility to your children. Firm discipline eliminates a large part of what is unpleasant in the parent-child relationship and establishes a structure in which both parents and children can operate to their best advantage. On the other hand lack of discipline brings about a constant friction between children and parents because no ground rules have been laid down. It is like playing baseball without any rules or any umpires. It results in chaos. But worse, this lack of definition causes a good many problems within the child that can ultimately lead to rebellions in school, drinking, drugs and other self-destructive forms of behavior.

COMMUNICATION

One of the most valuable legacies you can impart to your children is the ability to communicate. Communication is different from ordinary talking. Communication is the expression to another person of how you are *feeling*— either in general, about them, or about someone else. It should be distinguished from saying what you are *thinking* or from talking about some subject—such as politics, religion, the weather. Many people have great difficulty communicating. It appears that in America many, many children are specifically taught *not* to communicate. They are taught never to express to anyone what they feel, but to give an at best filtered, socially acceptable version of it. Parents are usually our role-models for communication or lack of it. However, our life experiences, including contacts with relatives, friends and, yes, therapists, can sometimes free us from this mold. Some of you readers may rarely communicate with anyone. Many of you do communicate with mates or close friends. Some of us find it harder to communicate much with children. Instead many parents may use some version of speech that either copies their parents or copies what the book they read said they should say or copies Robert Young in "Father Knows Best." Saying what you *feel* to a child is almost a social no-no. If you *are* one of the parents who does have honest communication with your mate, allow your child to be in on it whether it is love or anger that you are expressing. Be open with your child and keep as few secrets from him as possible.

The very best way to connect emotionally with your child is to tell him when you are anxious, upset, angry, sad, joyous, feel very loving toward him or wish he weren't there at that moment. Then something *real* is happening between the two of you instead of a sterile, routine, dead interchange. I am reminded of telephone conversations I have had with my children when I have been away from home. "How are you? How did it go in school today? Who did you play with? How did the game go? What are your plans for tomorrow? And the weekend?" What utter nonsense!!! Think how much more meaningful it would have been if I had said, "I feel very uncomfortable. I don't know what to say to you. This feels like a duty call. Actually all I really want to do is hear the sound of your voice." I am reminded of a patient of mine who was very, very anxious about approaching a woman and actually used to think out and even write down scripts that he could follow when he approached her. I told him that instead of that, he should tell the woman how terrified he felt on approaching her. This was so real and so honest that it evoked from her an immediate interest in him and made an emotional connection between them.

Communication is a two-way street. If you can do it, please do not curtail yourself because you think that it is bad for the child. Even a very hostile communication is much to be preferred to a false expression of love or concern or an emotional withdrawal. The other side of the coin is that you can encourage your child to express whatever he feels toward you, including the most hostile feelings even from the earliest years. If you set up a climate in which expression of any feeling is respected and rewarded, you will be aiding your child's ability to communicate. At times there is a fine line between communication and lack of respect, but this is a line that can be established. A child can say "I'm angry at you. I hate you. I feel at this moment as if I wish you were dead." That is different from saying "Drop dead." Even physical hostility can be encouraged, but it is best directed at a pillow or a Bo-bo doll as a stand-in rather than at your person. Physical violence either by a parent toward a child or by a child toward a parent rarely if ever accomplishes anything constructive.

A parent should not feel he must always appear to be kind, rational, heroic, good or fair to his child. Expressing his feelings in the presence of the child will make him appear to be more human and approachable and make the child more accepting of his own imperfections. It also helps him to separate from you because you are three-dimensional and not some God-like beneficient stereotype that he can never aspire to be and never aspire to find in another human being. Why should he leave you if you have presented yourself to him as the most wonderful person in the world, without any faults? And why should he risk leaving you and trying to attach himself to someone else when all they could be is very ugly in comparison to your perfection? Communication of feelings is far better and makes much more of an impact than lectures and sermons on honesty, the nature of life, morality and other such lofty (and to a child boring and irrelevant) issues.

Sometimes a child will come to you to express some feeling or discuss some problem when you are preoccupied with something else or tired. It is better for you to tell the child this and give him or her a future time rather than half-listen and pretend to go through the motions. This latter is very insulting and disappointing to a child and will tend to cut off future communications from him. When he does express himself, listen. If what he says does not interest you, be honest about it. If it does, praise him for telling you and give him an honest *feeling*—not thinking—response to it, good or bad.

The best policy to take with a child about health is a kind of studied neglect. Aside from a yearly routine check with the pediatrician or other type of physician, the less attention you can pay to bumps, bruises, scratches, stomach aches, irregularities in bowel function, low-grade fevers, sore throats, colds, and other minor ailments, the better. Even if you are unfortunate enough to be a hypochondriac yourself, try not to pass that on to your children. With rare exceptions, when a child is really sick, a layman will know it and will have enough sense to call a doctor. I have had two adult patients who were victimized by one or both of their parents' preoccupation with their health. Neither of them incidentally ever had any serious physical problem. Both of them are in excellent health today. When they were little girls, their parents dragged them from doctor to doctor. One of them had had a sister who died of rheumatic heart disease. She was taken to doctor after doctor looking for a heart murmur. Both girls grew up with a defective body image. They both felt that they were weak and unable to exert themselves as much as other people. This led one of them to give up trying to develop herself as a person and to fall into the role of wife and mother as if other challenges would be too much for her. Whenever she felt the slightest bit tired, she would quit and head for home. After years of analysis, she has launched a very successful and challenging professional career. But even after considerable therapy, both of these women tend to use preoccupation with their health to withdraw from life. You can do a great deal of harm to your child by focusing on minor physical troubles. This kind of attention can end up being more crippling than a real organic illness. If you find yourself being consistently overconcerned with your child's health, it is time for you to examine yourself and wonder what that is about. Many times overconcern of this kind is a reaction formation against some kind of unconscious hostility.

By this phrase psychoanalysts mean that parents who

harbor an *unconscious* hostility toward a child—for instance on the basis of seeing him as a rival for a mate or based on some other issue of which they are unaware—sometimes defend themselves against the hostility by going far over to the other end of things and being overconcerned or overprotective about their child's health and safety. However, this is not the only reason for overconcern. Overconcern can also be a way of binding a child to you by making him feel as if he cannot survive without you. This is one of the surest ways of retarding the "letting them go" process. I remember a strange coincidence of my going out on a date with a girl my father had treated for rheumatic heart disease. He was an excellent cardiologist, but unfortunately somewhat lacking as a psychiatrist. He had warned her and frightened her so severely about her physical limitations resulting from her heart problem that when she was in her twenties and I dated her, she was in excellent physical health but was an emotional cripple. We must be sure not to repeat this mistake as parents.

The same idea applies to overprotection in general. If you keep your child from riding a bicycle when other children do, from going to school alone when others do, from crossing streets, from going to camp, from having the same curfew as other children, what you are producing in the child is a feeling that he is not as strong, self-sufficient and responsible as others his age. You probably will not prevent any accident or anxiety. In fact the tension you create by your worry can bring about the very things you are trying to prevent. At times, in city life especially, a certain degree of caution about letting children out alone is warranted. You do not want your daughter to be raped or otherwise sexually molested and you do not want your sons or daughters to be mugged. It is difficult to find the exact line between being neglectful and being so concerned that you create unnecessary anxiety. In general I think you should try to keep your children out of dangerous situations in high crime areas and explain what the dangers are. But to try to prevent the danger by frightening them to death of the possibility of danger is unwise and causes more problems than it prevents. Attempts by mothers to warn daughters about the dangers of their being sexually molested sometimes help create fears and anxieties about sex in general. One of the same women with overanxious parents was frightened so much by her mother's warnings about sexual attacks that she developed severe phobias and inhibitions about sex and unconsciously reacted to every man she met as if he were the Boston Strangler. It is doubtful that excessive warnings have much effect in actually preventing these unfortunate events. It is better to view them as very rare and in most cases uncontrollable occurrences and not to produce undue anxiety in a child in what will be a fruitless attempt to ward off a very unlikely event.

However, this does not mean that, depending upon the neighborhood and the place where you live, it might not be extremely appropriate to warn the children without alarming them that they should not talk to or accept gifts from strangers, that they should never let a stranger into the house, that they should never take rides with strangers, and so on. This can be done in a way that confronts them with the realities of living in today's world (which includes a healthy skepticism and distrust of strangers) without frightening them so badly that they become paranoid or mistrustful or phobic.

ADMIRATION AND ADULATION

Even in the most sophisticated psychoanalytic circles narcissism up until recently has been a bit of a dirty word. Narcissism is a technical word for self-love. It comes from the legend of Narcissus, a Greek god who was so beautiful that he was fascinated by his reflection in a pond and died admiring himself. Narcissism has been defined as a preoccupation with oneself to the exclusion of interest in other people and other things. It manifests itself in a hypochondriacal attention to one's body, a preoccupation with one's physical attractiveness or the lack of it. Recently, especially due to the brilliant work of a psychoanalyst from Chicago, Dr. Heinz Kohut, we have achieved some new insights into the whole subject. Rather than just being

viewed as a sickness and an egocentricity, the need for
admiration and adulation is recognized as a basic human
need. The baby in the crib needs to see in his mother's face
the kind of adulation that defines him as the most marvelous, wonderful, beautiful thing that was ever created.
This is a response (granted an irrational, subjective one)
that many parents have and continue to have toward their
children, not only when they are babies—though especially then—but even as they grow up and become adults.
A developing person needs this kind of response. The
important thing is that getting this response from a parent
—especially in the first year of life but also later on—
rather than producing a narcissitic, egocentric, conceited
person, actually prevents it. The preoccupation with self
seen in some adults results from *not* having gotten enough
attention, admiration, and adulation from parents and
then needing to give this to themselves. They become so
involved in this process that they do not have enough
energy left to invest in other people or in the rest of the
world.

The important point for us to derive from these new
discoveries is that you do not spoil your child or make him
conceited by giving him genuine admiration and adulation. As a matter of fact the more of this you feel for him
and express to him, the better a self-image he will acquire
and the less preoccupied he will be with his body as an
adult. So be generous in sharing these feelings with your
child. These are not the feelings that bind him to you or
reduce his ability to be self-sufficient. The more you tell
your child he is beautiful, adorable, and lovable, the more
he will be apt to grow up that way and to be able to let
go of you and find someone else to love and be loved by.
He will carry the image of your mirroring him positively
in his mind and will not have to stop in front of every
mirror he passes to check to see if he is indeed a beautiful
person.

Whereas being "permissive" and vacillating about discipline and being overprotective can be very destructive to
a child, being adoring can be very helpful. Of course, if
you are *not* adoring, or if you find it hard to express those
kinds of feelings, it is better *not* to do it than to do it in

a false or forced way. That will just be sickening and will give the child nothing. Children can invariably tell when we are being genuine and when we are pretending. Pretending those feelings can be more destructive than not having them at all or not expressing them.

Another important issue concerning narcissism involves the shame so many people feel about their self-love. Nowadays most people have more trouble saying good things about themselves than they do talking about money, their intimate sexual experiences, or their bowel habits—the most usually acknowledged sources of shame. Often I have the members of therapy groups try to give a very short speech eulogizing themselves. The results are astounding. It is often impossible for any of them to say anything good about themselves. What they do say they qualify or manage to negate in the next sentence. I remember one fellow was so upset at the thought of such a speech that he ran out of the room crying rather than attempt it. Many of us are brought up to feel such shame about our self-love that we develop all sorts of symptoms or character traits because of it. Being conceited or swell-headed or grandiose appears to many of us to be the greatest sin of all.

I remember once a friend of mine introduced me at a party in complimentary terms to a friend of hers. My discomfort was so unbearable that I told her to say a bunch of rotten things about me to counter her original statement. She complied—perhaps *too* quickly and easily —and my discomfort ended. This may be an amusing anecdote but it has also been a very serious problem for me. I was so afraid to be grandiose that I really could never let in any good things or good reactions that came my way. Until this whole issue was analyzed, my self-esteem did not grow in any way from my earliest childhood on.

Another way shame about narcissism or exhibitionism manifests itself is with people who are painfully shy or have tremendous problems expressing themselves in classes or groups or social situations. This, as one can imagine, is tremendously inhibiting and disturbing. It is almost the rule rather than the exception for people to be quite anxious before performing or giving a speech. Many of these problems stem from being made to feel ashamed of a desire to exhibit oneself and receive adulation and praise. Remember, this is a perfectly normal and healthy desire.

Even if you do not feel adoring of your child or have trouble expressing it, at least you can attempt to spare him from feeling ashamed of desiring admiration and adulation. As an exercise try saying good things about yourself for two minutes in front of your mate or try getting your mate to say good things about you. You will discover quickly how well you have handled this issue.

Suppose you realize that you have not been sufficiently admiring of your child up until now and, in fact, may have made him feel ashamed of his even asking for this from you. Is there anything you can do to reverse the effects of the past? Well, the need for adulation is much greater in the early years than in the later ones, and the effect of not getting it early cannot be totally reversed. However, it will be very helpful if at any age you can begin to express a truly felt admiration for your child in a genuine, authentic way and to try to undo whatever shame you may have caused in him for having these needs for admiration. The fact is that the need for admiration is lifelong and the more we get the better it is for all of us!

PROMISES

Broken promises have an enormous impact on children as well as adults. I can remember well a patient who told me that his father had promised him he would bring back a Japanese submarine for him when he was discharged from the Army. This to his father was obviously a meaningless, harmless joke. To my patient at age six it represented one of the greatest disappointments in his life and seriously impaired any further trust he could have in his father. Breaking a promise to a child produces not only disappointment but usually hurt and sometimes rage. Worst of all, a broken promise creates a major erosion in the trust between a parent and child. I have seen adults who were sensitized as children by broken promises make serious suicide attempts at similar broken promises in their adult life. A promise to a child should never be made lightly, and the parent should be absolutely certain that he can and will fulfill it. Unless these conditions are met, it is extremely unwise to make a promise. You can say you hope to do such and such, but you cannot be completely sure. In that way you can still share the pleasure of future planning with your child without the dangers of a broken promise. Of course if you can make a definite decision, positive or negative, it is better to do so rather than leave the child hanging. The problem of trust is not simply that the child may not trust the parent. This lack of trust can be generalized so as to include everyone. It may take years of skillful psychotherapy to treat a person who after repeated broken promises and other negative experiences with his parents is unable to trust anyone including his therapist.

LYING AND STEALING

These problems are especially hard to deal with in an era in which many of the leaders of our government are constantly involved in both activities. It seems to me in general that one can get further with a pragmatic amoral approach than a condemning moralistic one. For one thing a condemning moralistic approach brings on a great deal of shame and humiliation, especially if the act is known to other members of the family or to friends. Condemnation usually results in a negative self-image. If you can show your child that lying and stealing do not pay, that honesty is really the best policy without resorting to assassinating his character, he is more likely to be receptive to your admonitions. However, if you yourself operate in a very moralistic framework, then you must impose your particular views on your child. You must be true to yourself, and you cannot present an argument from a pragmatic point of view when you basically see the issue as a moral one.

Though this rule does not hold absolutely true all of the time, if a child lies or steals, he is probably either using you as a model or else there is some severe disruption in the parent-child relationship. If you brag about how you came out ahead by lying to a customer or walk home from the office with your arms full of pencils, pens, stationery and practically everything that is not nailed down, don't be too surprised if your child follows your example. Don't forget, you are his model, and he is flattering you by imitating you. He doesn't realize that you could possibly be doing anything wrong.

But if you are a sterling character in every possible way and your child steals either from you or from someone else, the chances are he is either imitating a close friend or a gang, or else he is suffering from some sense of emotional deprivation. It might be wise to try to figure out what is going on emotionally that might express itself in the symptom of stealing. This does not mean being "soft" on it or condoning it, but it does mean paying a good deal of attention to the symptom and to the child that exhibits the symptom. Sometimes the answer will not be too difficult to find. Perhaps the child feels his sibling has been favored too consistently. He may even be correct in his perceptions.

Lying to you also has to indicate some exaggerated fear or lack of trust in you. When you discover it, you must raise the question in your own mind about what you have conveyed in your attitude that caused the child to lie. You should have several heart-to-heart talks with the child not only about what is pragmatically or—if you will—morally wrong about lying in general but also about the fact that there must be something wrong in your relationship to your child that has brought this about. It is very helpful if you can get the child to tell you what it is about *you* that brought about the lie as well as what it is about himself that did.

Up until age four, children rarely lie in the usual sense of our use of the word. Rather the child tends to live more in his imagination and make up stories. At this age many children delight in fairy tales and love to hear stories made up by their mothers or fathers. Stretching the truth a bit or even a good deal is more apt to be a function of creative imagination than of a serious problem. For the older child chronic lying is a response to some difficulty in the parent-child relationship. Of course, an occasional white lie is not to be taken seriously, but can be a pragmatic and even appropriate way of smoothing over a difficult situation.

Small children up to age four do not really steal. Rather they do not have a clear sense of what belongs to them and what belongs to others. They generally know what they want and take it. From age six on the child clearly knows these distinctions. Stealing is especially common around age seven and in early adolescence. At these ages the child is usually growing up and growing away from parents, and he may go through a period in which he feels lonely since he may not have established strong peer relationships. It is a good thing for parents not to leave money around to offer too easy a temptation to children of these ages. Children who steal often use the money to buy friendship by giving other children the money directly or by buying candy and presents for them. Stealing in general represents some feeling of unfulfilled need. Sometimes it may represent going along with a model that a playmate or a group sets. Of course, the bad companion theory can be stretched. I remember a psychiatrist on the children's ward saying to me, "Every mother who brings her child in here always blames his problems on bad companions. How come we never see the bad companions here?" However, gang stealing in adolescence is not necessarily as reflective of a severe parent-child problem. It may be based more on the child's need to conform to a group and establish himself as one of them. Of course, in some of today's young people there is an ethic that *unless* one steals from the establishment one is immoral. Many young people consistently steal from stores and groceries. This kind of stealing, while it clearly shows evidence of society's ills and disruption, is not necessarily or even usually a sign of personal difficulty or parent-child problems. However, if you do not share your children's view of stealing from the establishment, you must deal with this problem as *you* view it.

I think that allowances should be instituted as early as possible—say age five—to encourage a sense of autonomy and responsibility. It also eliminates the humiliation of the child's having to go to the parent and ask (or perhaps beg) for money for each little thing that comes up. This situation creates tension between parent and child and hostility in both. It tends to perpetuate a dependent relationship that lacks dignity. On the other hand, the advantages of the child's having an allowance are quite obvious. There is one domain in which he is in absolute and total control. He is completely responsible for being able to make the most for himself out of the money allotted to him. It teaches him to plan and to make choices constantly. This reinforces a feeling of his power and the fact that his choices have consequences—negative and positive— that are his and only his responsibility. The allowance itself creates a clear, real separation between what is his as distinct from what belongs to his parents. It is one of the most effective ways of helping to bring about an emotional separation—of letting go—between the child and the parents.

It must be clearly and openly understood that the allowance is a privilege and not a right. Withholding the allowance or docking a certain amount of the allowance is one of the most effective means of enforcing discipline. It is relatively painless and free from elements of humiliation, and yet it is a very powerful way of setting and enforcing limits and punishing transgressions. It should be used as frequently as is necessary. One of the parents' strongest powers is the power of the purse. They should use it openly and without guilt or apologies to enforce what they believe to be a just structure. This is no more than using punishment as part of the application of learning theory to help extinguish unacceptable behavior. If this is done consistently and even minor infractions are punished by docking a token amount of allowance, undesirable behavior will be controlled and will not escalate into more drastic rebellions later on which include alcohol, drugs, breaking the law, and so on. It is tremendously important to set up a system of firm controls while your child is still young and malleable. Then when he reaches adolescence, this pattern will already exist in your relationship, and you will be able to deal with the expected rebellious behavior in a way that will keep it from getting totally out of hand. Adolescents who stray too far off the mark and get involved in all sorts of self-destructive behavior usually have parents who have either vacillated or abdicated their role or at times even unconsciously encouraged rebellious behavior in their children.

The amount of allowance should depend upon the age of your child and the "standard of living" of his peers. Check around to see what the usual allowance is for his peers. Then use your own judgment; you do not have to follow the pack. They might be wrong or their views might not coincide with your views or your income. In general you must try to set the allowance at some realistic figure, not so low that the child has to come to you constantly anyway and not so high that the child has so much money he does not have to bother to plan and choose. The more you can make the child responsible for—the more the allowance covers—the better it is. So allowances should cover such things as movies, sports events, games, sports equipment, extra foods and carfare as soon as the child's age dictates this.

Allowances should also cover, at the earliest possible age, money for clothing. This is a tremendously important method of encouraging independence from you and giving the child the greatest amount of responsibility for choice. The age at which this is instituted will vary somewhat from child to child. Certainly this does not apply to a six year old. But it may very well apply to a mature twelve year old. Not many parents think of instituting a clothing allowance for a child of that age. You should decide how much over a year, let us say, you can afford to spend on a particular child's clothing. As soon as possible you can leave it to him to decide what clothing he needs and what style he chooses. This will begin to give him a sense of his individuality. So many patients I see—patients who have never effectively made the emotional separation from their parents—are completely out of touch with their own preferences. As an exercise I give them a complete blank check, and many of them are totally unable to fill in anything. They have no idea what they want or even that there is a self with unique wants and desires. I often have to start them off by asking them a question such as, "What do you prefer—French-fried potatoes or mashed potatoes? Vanilla or chocolate ice cream? Symphonic music or rock?" Strangely enough they frequently cannot even answer these questions. The whole idea of having or being a separate, unique individual has never occurred to them. Naturally, then, what the preferences of this particular individual are has also never occurred to them. These people go through life following the dictates of the herd or of whatever individual or group they may be connected with at any particular time. Even though they may appear outwardly to be successful in their professional, social or sexual life, they are going through someone else's motions rather than being self-directing. They go through life without really being alive. It is as though they are still in their mother's womb and have never severed the umbilical cord. These people may seem to be perfectly normal, well-functioning adults by any objective standard. Yet subjectively they almost do not experience themselves as existing. I am not describing bizarre, psychotic people. I am describing a part of almost all of us that functions on automatic controls and loses touch with our power to choose and make decisions. This depends on the degree of emotional separation we have achieved from our parents. And "our parents" should not be taken too literally. Even if both of our parents are dead and have been so for a long time, this does not mean that we have achieved emotional separation. The connection is merely transferred to a mate, a boss, an older sibling, an organization, or even a society, whose norms and values we accept unquestioningly. In the process we abdicate our own individuality. This has the "advantage" of our never having to make a decision, but the disadvantage that we are hardly ever going to get what we really want or what really pleases us because we haven't ever been in touch with what it is. Even when we know what we want and apply all of our will and power toward getting it, we may very well fail. If we don't even know what it is, the chances of our getting it become infinitesimal.

Thus, you can see how important the allowance is in establishing an autonomous self in the child—not, of course, by itself alone, but as part of a total program of pushing independence. Included in the system of allowances should be encouragement of the children, at as early an age as possible, to open their own bank accounts. This certainly gives them a sense of separateness from you. Along with the allowance system, the child must be responsible for having enough money on hand when he needs it. He should not be permitted to borrow from you, unless there is truly an exceptional and unforeseen circumstance. Otherwise, all of the good effects of the allowance will be abrogated. The same applies to dealing with gifts of money from relatives. Some well-meaning grandparents or other relatives can completely disrupt the system by constantly feeding the children money. This gift money must be controlled through the parents. It may, for instance, be set aside in a fund for some special purpose that requires a large expenditure, but it obviously cannot merely be added indiscriminately to the allowance and used by the child. This is one of the most frequent saboteurs of the system. A parent feels a bit Scrooge-like in taking away the dollar that Grandpa gave Johnny. Johnny will be outraged too and so will Grandpa unless the total idea is explained carefully to everyone.

Of course the amount of allowance must be determined by the parents' own economic state, but if this changes (if a parent loses a job, for instance), the allowance should be cut proportionately.

If you have not instituted a system of allowances yet and find yourself agreeing with my general thesis, then by all means do so at the earliest possible moment. Better late than never, in this case. Explain to your child that you have heard that this system works well and you plan to try it.

In any case, I cannot emphasize too much how impor-

tant this whole system of allowances is to the development of your child. Do not avoid this; it is too crucial.

—————————————————HOUSEHOLD DUTIES AND CHORES

Another activity that encourages development of an autonomous, independent self is the institution of household duties at as early an age as possible. Even at age three there are certain duties such as care of personal belongings, dressing, brushing one's hair, washing oneself, putting away toys, putting away clothing, that a child can begin to do. By five children can be learning to set the table and carrying their own belongings on trips, all of which can give them a sense of their own power and effectiveness. By six they should be able to put themselves to bed. They should be able to brush their teeth, undress, put on their pajamas and be ready for Mom or Dad to read or tell them a story and kiss them good night.

All children, both male and female, should be made to participate in all aspects of running a home—buying food, cooking, washing, cleaning, straightening up, garbage disposal, gardening, snow removal, and so forth. This is one important way to avoid a male chauvinist orientation. Treating girls and boys alike in this respect, without distinctions in duties on the basis of sex, will go a long way toward making an important inroad on what I believe to be one of the most destructive attitudes in our culture—male chauvinism. I remember very clearly that my father at age fifty did not even know in what closet the cups were kept. He boasted that in his whole life he had never been to a store to buy a quart of milk and he had never boiled water. But my father, though he was an extremely competent and successful physician, was totally helpless as far as taking care of himself. This total helplessness obviously had to result in a persistent anxiety as well as in a necessity to enslave and dominate a woman so as to be sure he had a constant servant. The results of this are all too well known to most of us—a mutually sado-masochistic relationship that brings great suffering to both partners, to the sadist as well as the masochist.

Getting back to household duties and chores: a mother is obviously not doing her children any good by being their servant or incidentally by having her servant or servants be their servant. She is depriving them of a rare opportunity to feel truly self-sufficient about taking care of their basic daily needs. No matter how expert one may be in some highly specialized profession, it is essential to have the ability, and the knowledge of having the ability, to handle basic needs without seeking outside assistance. There may be a problem for some when there is a maid in the house. The children will obviously expect to be waited on and served just as their parents are by servants. The maid may expect to do this as well. In these circumstances it is important for the parent to explain carefully both to the children and to the maid the rationale for *not* doing this. They may grumble a bit, but it is better for them in the long run.

It is implicit that the household tasks chosen should be within the physical, neurological, and emotional ability of the child to perform. Otherwise both child and parent will be frustrated. The task should not simply be given as a learning experience but as a realistic and authentic aid to the parent and the family. If there is uncertainty about the child's ability to perform, then a task can be tried and *postponed* (not abandoned) if it appears too formidable.

In addition to household chores, as soon as possible, starting at age eleven or twelve, children should be strongly encouraged to supplement their allowance by baby-sitting, snow removal, delivery for stores, having a paper route, and other independent activities. The sooner they get the feeling of being able to earn their own money through their own efforts, the sooner they will be able to break the ties from you. There may be jobs around the house that involve a special effort such as painting or cleaning for which an outside person would have to be hired. When they are old enough to be capable of doing a good job, give them the opportunity to make extra money by working for you and pay them a fair wage for their efforts. This applies too to baby-sitting for smaller

children. Older children who would have the opportunity
to be out with their friends will correctly resent having to
stay home to baby-sit for younger siblings. It will create
hostility toward you and toward the younger sibling. My
daughter used to express this resentment toward her
younger brother (I found out many years later) by perpe-
trating subtle and not so subtle acts of sadism toward him,
such as putting ice cubes down his clothing, breaking eggs
over his head (under the guise of giving him an egg sham-
poo) and some others too horrible to recall or mention.
Especially if the older sibling is being paid to baby-sit for
someone else, it is unfair to expect him or her to do it for
you for nothing. The child will make you pay for it in one
way or another. There is no such thing as a "built-in
baby-sitter." This practice just augments whatever sibling
rivalry problems may already exist.

The institution of household chores, then, is another
basic and important cornerstone in helping your children
become separate people. If you have not given them these
chores yet, by all means begin now. You can honestly say
to them that you have been doing some reading and
thinking about it, and perhaps you have been mistaken in
the past and you wish to make some changes now. There
is no reason for your child to think you don't make mistakes.

————————HOMEWORK AND SCHOOL MARKS

It is important that you be clear on what you want from
your child in relationship to scholastic performance. How
your child does in school may or may not matter to you.
But one way or the other you should know where you
stand honestly and communicate it directly to your child.
Some parents, including myself unfortunately, have told
their children that marks and getting into a good college
really did not matter, that what mattered was one's social
adjustment and personal happiness. But though I really
believed I meant this, in retrospect I can see now that it
was not true. I would like to have meant it, but I had been
too caught up in academic success myself to be able to

dismiss easily a son of mine getting anything but superior marks. My son has chided me correctly for spouting the philosophy that marks didn't count and then being very disappointed when he didn't get into Harvard. He was very disappointed too, which meant he received the unconscious message as well as the overt one. Actually what happened resulted in a real confusion that is produced by what is known as a *double bind*. A double bind is created when a parent gives off two messages that are mutually exclusive. Sometimes these messages are both said overtly like, "Be kind and considerate to people" and "Be sure to be aggressive and always get what you want," or "Don't take any baloney from your teachers" and "Get A's in conduct," or "Success isn't important" and "Why aren't you first in your class?" In any case my double bind was consciously, "Marks don't count" and covertly, "You must get excellent marks." Double binds have very disastrous effects on people in general and children in particular. A double bind tends to immobilize or paralyze one. There is no right thing to do since the commands are totally incompatible. It is as though a sergeant were saying to his men "Right face" and "Left face" at the same time. One way to confuse a child is to tell him not to bother about grades when it really matters to you. The other is to pretend a great interest in school marks and success when in fact you couldn't care less, never help with homework, hardly glance at report cards and really have your mind completely on your latest golf score.

Once you have decided what you want or don't care about, then you can communicate this honestly to your children. Don't pretend one way or the other. If you are interested in their scholastic achievement, then it is appropriate to keep asking how they are doing and to check up, to a point, on whether they are doing their homework. But you can't in good conscience do this if you aren't also willing to help them with homework occasionally—not do it for them or supply the answers but discuss the principles behind it, go to open school week and PTA meetings, put in the time that backs your position of interest. If you take this position, you should try not to be a constant nag about homework, but merely to show an interest. Here too within the framework *you* set, you should try to allow the child to be as autonomous as possible. This is especially true in helping with homework. It is a lot easier most of the time merely to supply the child with the answer without going through a whole explanation of the idea behind it. But this is binding your child and making him dependent. You want to teach him the idea so that *he* will be able to arrive at the answer himself with this particular question and with future questions that resemble it.

If you really couldn't care less how your child does in school, he might in the long run be better off. Because then he will not have the burden of either working to please you or *not* working to rebel against you. He will just be following his natural interest and bent and will be likely to work at his optimum depending upon the skill of his teacher in arousing and maintaining his interest.

If marks really don't matter to you, be honest about it with your children. When they show you their report cards, make it clear that your lack of enthusiasm or failure to be appalled comes out of a value system in which marks and scholastic performance do not have a very high priority. You can explain to them what issues of theirs or your own have higher priorities, such as ability to socialize, excellence in sports, religious attitude or whatever else they may be.

If a child has a high or at least an adequate I.Q. and keeps on failing, this is indicative of some emotional problem for which professional help should be sought at least in terms of diagnosing the problem. Incidentally I.Q. tests have a fairly good percentage of validity. Occasionally I have seen I.Q.s that were significantly lowered by severe emotional problems, but even here a good tester can and will usually report that the scatter among the subtests indicates that there is a potential for a much higher I.Q.

The standard Wechsler-Bellevue Intelligence test breaks down intelligence into many different categories. There is a broad division between verbal intelligence and performance intelligence. But then there are many further breakdowns into categories such as being able to repeat a series of digits forward and backward, vocabulary, general information and others. Usually one of the subtests or more is not so markedly affected by emotional problems, so even in a test showing the I.Q. generally lowered, there are subtests which may score very high that give an indication of what the child's potential may be.

It might be wise at this juncture to mention that I.Q. tests have been attacked from many points of view as not really valid indications of a person's intellectual potential. One accurate attack is that these tests were standardized for middle-class white American children and their validity for black children or children who come from other cultures inside America or homes in which English is not the only language spoken is questionable.

I.Q.s have been a poorly kept secret for many children. I see no harm in a child with a high I.Q. knowing that he has superior endowment. There might be a better case made out for keeping a low I.Q. score from a child, but even this might not clearly follow. Having a good idea of what one's endowment is may be useful in helping one to make realistic choices and decisions about the type of school program and vocational goals one should pursue. I see no harm in sharing an I.Q. with a twelve year old.

Children from intellectually competitive homes usually worry a great deal more about their scholastic achievements. On the other hand, they also usually achieve more. It would be nice to have the latter without the former, but obviously one cannot have it both ways. Fortunately or unfortunately you and your attitudes are going to set the tone for many of your child's responses in this area. You might as well try to be straight with yourself and with your child about how you really feel about his schoolwork.

EXTRACURRICULAR ACTIVITIES: MUSIC AND DANCE LESSONS, ATHLETICS

I like to give my own family's story as an example when the question comes up about music lessons. I love jazz and can't stand classical music. But the kind of music I really abhor is opera. It is an absolute impossibility for me to stay awake through a whole opera. I maintain that if someone wanted to get me to reveal atomic secrets, all they would have to do would be to put me in a room with an operatic soprano. So I practically forbade any music in the house. When my children requested piano lessons, I turned them down on it continually until they begged so hard that I finally had to relent. Well, the end of the story as you may guess is that despite the fact that there has been no evidence of musical talent in my family or my wife's for generations, two of my children have graduate degrees in music and both have become opera singers. I say that they figured out the way they could get me where it hurt the most. And sure enough my daughter is an operatic soprano and my son an operatic tenor. Of course, even when I watch them perform, I have a hard time staying awake.

So when parents ask me how they can awaken their children's interest in taking piano lessons (or even becoming amateur or professional musicians), I tell them my story. I think it has a real point. I am sure that if my children had been pushed or forced to take piano lessons, they would have hated them and they would have become tap dancers. If I had only been smart enough to figure that out then! The psychological point is that in the process of having to fight for something they wanted against their parents' wishes, they found a way of expressing a desire that had by force to come out of themselves. Becoming opera singers one might say was a rebellion against me. But actually that is a rather foolish and simplistic explanation. Even if there might have been an initial push brought about by rebellion, it could certainly not have sustained all the arduous hours of work necessary to achieve the skill it takes to be a performer or the ability to transcend all of the heartbreaks and disappointments along the way. One reason why they were able to commit themselves so totally to this field is that their choice, especially the eldest's, was clearly her own individual unique choice, not copied from anyone. It had the effect of distinguishing her from anyone else in the family and constantly reaffirming her individuality and separateness.

The moral of this whole story is that, while there may be some value in exposing your children to all kinds of cultural and artistic and athletic experiences so they will be able to choose which of them happens to be *their* cup of tea, it is really unwise to push a child into any of these areas. It is better for the desire for whatever form of expression your child chooses to arise out of him rather than for him to become a narcissistic extension of yourself and a vehicle through whom you will try to fulfill your own frustrated artistic or athletic aspirations. I have had so many patients who were pushed in various artistic directions by their parents. They were apparently brilliant and talented, but ultimately, when they began an emotional separation from their parents, they gave up the whole thing. One of my patients was a brilliant concert pianist at age nineteen. He gave it up completely, became a successful rock musician for a while and then gave up music completely to become a psychotherapist. Now he will never touch a piano. This is more typical than atypical among my patient population. I have an adult patient, a frustrated athlete who was pushing his son to become a baseball player. He became the manager of his Little League baseball team and was very involved with his son's progress. His son, a mediocre player at best, was becoming very uncomfortable about all this and was showing signs of hostility and rebellion toward him. At my advice the next year my patient cooled his interest in his son's athletic career and gave up managing his Little League team. His son's hostility to him stopped and they get along much better now.

The concept of a child's being *a narcissistic extension* of a parent is a very important one for parents to know and understand. What the term means literally is that the child is perceived as an extension of our own self-love rather than as a human being who is different from, separate from ourselves. I feel that almost all of us parents have some degree of this kind of thing operating in relation to our children. If all it involves is that we are proud of them and take pleasure in their accomplishments, that is a normal parental reaction and can give them the kind of adoration and adulation they need, as mentioned above. But often a different development takes place that is very destructive for both parent and child: if this occurs, we begin to pin on the child the longings and hopes for accomplishment—scholastic, financial, artistic, athletic, social—that we have never been able to achieve ourselves. Then we lose touch with who our child really is, what his particular bents, talents, and interests are. We superimpose our own goals upon him and then react to the child as if they were his. Stage mothers who push their children's careers, such as the mother in *Gypsy,* are good examples of this. Children who have been pushed by parents in this way usually have all sorts of problems and end up feeling used and negated (which they have been) by their parents.

The point of all this is that when you start giving your child piano lessons or ballet lessons or karate lessons or enroll him in the Little League, try to figure out whether this is something *he* has chosen or if you have subtly chosen it for him because you are a frustrated Paderewski or Nijinsky or Ted Williams. Another reason you may have chosen it is that you are using your children to compete against other children, so you can—through them—compete with other parents. In a competitive society such as ours, this is often a major issue with parents. The term "child wearers" is a good one that covers the idea of the child being both a narcissistic extension and a pawn in the competition with other adults. Both ways he is being negated as a person and used by you.

If he has really chosen his sport or art or music—almost despite you—it can be of tremendous value in his becoming an autonomous self who has character and distinction and is not just a carbon copy. If you have imposed it on him, then whatever values the activity may have intrinsically, the total effect will be very destructive for your child and will ultimately generate hostility toward you. So, if you have gotten him to take piano lessons and he keeps sneaking off to play ball instead of practicing, you'd better forget about it. It is more important for him to be a person than a pianist.

Perhaps the only situation in which it may be allowable to push a child "athletically"—and this is a very special case—is when the school feels that he has some specific gross motor or fine motor deficit and that some "learning disability" training may be helpful to him. "Learning disability" training is a rather new term for a relatively new and as yet rather vaguely defined specialty that covers remedial work with children who have minor, difficult-to-detect, neurological impairment that may affect their motor skills, especially in athletics, and their reading, language or other skills. Sometimes, especially if the detection is early—from nursery to the first or second grade—a little help along these lines can go a long way. If you find your child has some minor disability in any of these areas, it might be wise to investigate it either through the school or through your pediatrician. It is important to try to catch the disability as early as possible. By the time the child enters kindergarten or first grade, the difference between him and other children will become apparent to him. He will feel like some sort of cripple or freak even if he finds he cannot play hopscotch as well as the other children. This will damage his self-image and bring on the emotional problems that follow that. So it really pays to bring any such possibility to the attention of your pediatrician. Some telltale signs are a child's going up or down stairs without alternating feet, inability to catch a large ball, and difficulty in hopping on one foot. The way children hold pencils, crayons, spoons and forks—grabbing them clumsily instead of holding them at the appropriate ages—are other signs.

CHOICE OF FRIENDS

As I reported above, when I was working on the child psychiatry ward of Bellevue Hospital, the Chief of Service, the famous child psychiatrist, Dr. Loretta Bender, said, "Parents are constantly saying that their children arrived on this ward because of bad companions. How come we never get any of their bad companions here?"

Actually I think bad companions *can* have a very deleterious influence on children. Children are open and developing and do a great deal of identifying with the people around them. Unfortunately they do not have the opportunity to choose their parents; they are stuck with us for better or for worse. They are certainly going to take into themselves some of our better as well as our worst features. Who we become as people in some ways is a patchwork quilt of what we have taken in from various people we have encountered superimposed on our genetic and constitutional endowment. But whereas we cannot choose their parents and relatives, we certainly can exercise an influence over their choice of friends. Now, it may seem arbitrary and in opposition to the general thesis of this book to invade their autonomy and dictate who their friends should or should not be. In truth there is a danger and a deficit in interfering too strongly with their choices of playmates. On the other hand, we must balance this against what may be a greater deficit in not taking a stand against or at least exerting discouraging influences against certain friends who really do appear to be bad companions who exert unhealthy influences on our children in terms of identification. Now exactly *what* is unhealthy is very much a subjective matter that will vary from parent to parent. But whatever it is that *you* see as an unhealthy influence from a friend, you might be better off trying to discourage the friendship than allowing it to flourish. Conversely, if your child has a friend who would, in your opinion, exert a good influence on your child, you can reinforce the friendship by saying good things about the child, encouraging invitations, and being welcoming when that child is in your home.

Let me give you two examples. My five-year-old daughter began to play with a little girl who was extremely bratty, tremendously indulged and overprotected by her parents. On the days my daughter played with her she came home a carbon copy of this impossible brat! This was very much in contrast to her usual behavior. Though we did not prohibit her playing with this child, we expressed our negative feelings toward the child's behavior openly to our daughter, did *not* invite the child to come and play at our house, and politely declined invitations from this child's parents to go to her house for lunch, sleep-overs, and the like. Our daughter still plays with this child occasionally but much less frequently and our daughter now comments frequently on what a bratty, unpleasant child she is and how she really prefers playing with other children.

When our son was twelve years old, he became involved with a gang of children at school who were smoking marijuana heavily. I will go into my feelings about this in a later section, but they are obviously pretty negative—especially for twelve year olds. Some of the members of this gang were so involved in smoking that they had set up a whole "religious" code built around it, undoubtedly following Carlos Castaneda. We were very much alarmed about our son's continued association with these boys. In this case, we absolutely prohibited him from ever having any of them over to our house or from receiving phone calls from them. We restricted his going out at night or on weekends. We explained in detail our whole rationale and our feelings about smoking marijuana. He was very hurt and angry about these restrictions and for a while he continued to see these boys at school during the day. We did not attempt to restrict this, realizing that in reality we could not prevent such contact with them. But within a period of several months, our pressure paid off: our son's contact with these boys ceased, dying a natural death, and our son had a whole new group of acquaintances, none of whom were smoking marijuana.

The moral of these stories is that children do in fact introject, that is, take into themselves, traits of their peers. Children are very malleable and have all kinds of choices and directions in which they can go. If you see your child going with a child who is an especially bad model in *your* view—bratty, whining, on drugs or alcohol, anti-social, destructive—you have the power and the right and the responsibility to influence your child's choice of companions. You should always explain clearly to your child what you are doing and why. You should do this without being any more intrusive in trampling on his ego boundaries and his rights as an individual than is necessary. But you have to judge which is the biggest danger or deficit in any one particular situation. Remember that your child will be constantly in the process of taking in pieces of the people around him, including pieces of you. Remember also that you can exert pressure and influence on a child up to a certain age, diminishing as his age increases. Once past a certain age, it is too late. What we were able to do with a twelve year old, we could not have done with a seventeen year old. Remember that you are the parent and it is your responsibility as well as your right to be in charge and to use your power in the way you see fit to help your child develop into the adult you want him to be. Allowing your child to associate with people who, in your opinion, exert a bad influence on him is abdicating your responsibility and not being helpful to your child. Again, this advice is based on the fact that you, the parent, *are in charge.*

TOYS, COMICS, MAGAZINES, BOOKS, AND MOVIES

Many of us have a problem with how much leeway we should give our children in choosing their toys, comics, movies, books, and the like. Most of us want to encourage as much individuality as possible to help ourselves and the child in the letting go process. However, many of us have rather strong convictions, let us say against war and violence, against certain forms of sexual expression, or, for example, either for or against girls playing only with dolls and boys with erector sets. Sometimes the line is blurred between being autocratic and dictatorial, censoring the child so much as to inhibit freedom of an appropriate interest, and trying to foster what we consider healthy attitudes in our children. In regard to comics, so many of them—even those geared toward young children—are filled with violence. Is this harmful? Does it tend toward making them violent adults or at least adults who are more prone to condone violence? Some psychiatrists, notably Dr. Frederic Wertham, feel that these comics can be a very deleterious influence. I personally feel that there is so much violence constantly being shown in all news media, television, books, and movies that to escape it or protect your child from it would be tantamount to either locking him in his room or moving out of the country. On the other hand, there may be simple choices that we as parents can make rather unobtrusively, such as not getting Johnny toy soldiers or a machine gun or a tomahawk for his fifth birthday present. In another section I will describe the influence we can exert over television viewing. We can also do this about movies. PG (Parental Guidance Suggested) rated movies make it possible for us to exert complete control, and we can forbid other movies outright. Without being overly harsh censors, we can also exert an influence over choice of comics, books, and magazines, at least till the age of twelve. (Of course, if you genuinely feel you should exert this influence as long as your children live at home, then you should do so.)

It seems to me we are better off being authentic people with clear likes and dislikes and unashamedly attempt to impose them on our children. If the children disagree and object, they can find ways of expressing themselves that do not come under our direct surveillance. In seeing our points of view clearly—even if mother's and father's views differ on occasion—they will have a firm structure that they will later accept or reject on the basis of their own individuality. As I have repeated so often in other sections, the most damaging thing to a developing child is for him not to know what you really think or feel about things, nor should he feel that you are merely an extension of his own wishes. I think that if you err, it is better to err in the direction of too much control over these areas of your child's life rather than too little.

FATHER'S INVOLVEMENT

As readers already know, I consider myself a dedicated feminist. Not all feminists have necessarily or consistently welcomed me into their ranks, but at least in my own subjective view I feel that I espouse feminist ideas and goals. Now feminists have made a very strong point about the involvement of the father in the rearing of children from birth on. In theory I agree with them. I think the infant's and child's experiencing of closeness with two parents rather than one helps to prevent some of the sticky mother-child binds that tend all too frequently to develop and may make the letting go more difficult. I also feel that an equal division of household chores and child-rearing will ultimately lead to a woman's being able to develop and express her talent, creativity, and potential in the same ways that a man has the opportunity to do at present. Being more involved in child-rearing is apt to make a man more human, softer and more sensitive. This helps undo the strong, silent stereotype role that many men feel bound to play in our society. In addition the father would have the opportunity to experience some of the rich personal rewards and pleasures that many of them are now denied by our present social structure. I feel very strongly that an increase in the father's participation in the family and in child-rearing should be encouraged in every possible way. I fervently hope that after a few more generations there will be a drastic change in our family structure as well as in male-female relationships. I think that our present structure—even with the minor changes that have certainly begun to occur in the past five or ten years—still leaves a great deal to be desired. Women are still oppressed and find it very difficult to achieve a sense of equality with men or the opportunity to express their creative potential.

Nevertheless, while I am so sympathetic to these goals, I realize that we are now just beginning a period of transition. Many men have been so brought up in and indoctrinated with male chauvinist ideas that they will not be able to transcend all of their past acculturation. To try to cast a dedicated male chauvinist into a feminist mold is simply ridiculous. Hopefully, education, modeling from some of his friends, influences from the mass media *and* pressure from his wife (and children) will begin to have their gradual effect.

But I believe everyone is entitled to his individuality—even unfortunately his male chauvinist individuality. Therefore, each father must determine the degree of involvement he can and will have in rearing his child. He should know that in general the more involvement he wishes to have, the better it will be for the child and probably for himself. But his involvement must come out of a real *feeling* on his part—not out of copying a supposedly ideal father in a TV situation comedy or out of trying to fit into a feminist ideal that he cannot achieve. Again the important point is that anything that is forced or unnatural will not do anyone any good. At the same time hopefully more men will at least be induced to experiment with a greater degree of involvement in child-rearing. Try it, you'll like it. Or maybe you won't, but at least you will have tried.

Some of the recent work in child development seems to indicate the need of an infant in the first year of life for a relationship with *one* figure who is consistently there. Of course, this research itself may grow out of an orientation that is male chauvinist. There is nothing to indicate that this relationship has to be with the mother rather than the father. There is just such a paucity of material about children being raised from birth by a man. It might work out very well. But we are not yet ready to suggest that the father's involvement with the infant should necessarily supplant the mother's or substitute for it. Rather it could be *in addition to* it rather than *instead* of it. How this will work out in the distant future if and when feminist ideas really take hold in a very basic way is for now a matter of pure speculation. For the time being it may be a good idea if the father started to share in some of the feeding of the baby from the bottle (if it is used) on up and also share in diapering and responding to the crying at night during the first year. I cannot see the father *supplanting* the mother in these areas unless there is a very unusual situation of severe maternal illness. But I do think the introduction of the father into these situations gradually from the first days after birth on up would probably work out well for the child. I have been witness to two such situations. In one the father was a writer who spent a great deal of time at home, and in the other he was a free-lance graphic artist who did his work at home. In one instance the child was a delight and a joy. In the other the child was an impossible brat. However, the variable was clearly the quality of mothering that the mother was able to supply. In one instance the mother was warm and loving; in the other she was anxious, immature, and narcissistic. Certainly after the first year of life, during which I personally —and perhaps, I admit, incorrectly—feel that the preponderance of the child's contact should be with the mother, the more the father is present and involved with the child, the better. The child needs an alliance with the father (or with a sibling) to help negotiate the "letting go" process from the mother. Obviously the more the father is involved with the child after the first year, the better it is for the child. But as I have said repeatedly, this also depends on the quality of the feeling response of the father. If the father hates every minute he spends with the child and is doing it out of duty, he is not doing his child or himself any favors.

I remember spending several hours of pure hell dragging my children to amusement parks and circuses. I *hate* amusement parks and circuses. After several years of this —I was obviously *not* a fast learner—I began to realize what a farce this was. I usually was mad enough to spit, and my children were not unaware of my fury. The day was a disaster for all of us. Eventually I decided that if I spent time with my children, it should be at an activity that I truly enjoyed. So we began to go to zoos—I love zoos—and botanical gardens—like Ferdinand, I love flowers—and occasionally to baseball and basketball games, which I admit I probably liked a lot more than they did. But at least our time together was no longer sheer hell. I realized that I had to enjoy what we were doing for them to enjoy it.

The whole area of the father's involvement in child-rearing constitutes material for a book in itself.

TELEVISION

There are many views pro and con about the impact of television on children. Whether you are for it or against it, you cannot deny the enormous influence that it has on children. On the positive side, it has certainly made children a great deal more sophisticated about the world at a much earlier age than they would ordinarily be. It has literally brought into their living rooms and their lives all sorts of situations and people that they would otherwise not meet. On the negative side it makes them prey to constant propaganda that tends to reinforce establishment ideas and perhaps limit their own imagination, fantasy and ultimately creativity and individuality. It has made ten year olds sexually sophisticated. It has also exposed children to constant violence. Some psychiatrists consider this to be a seriously deleterious influence, whereas others say that violence is part of being human anyway and witnessing it on television does not have any major impact on a child. My own views are probably not worth any more than anyone else's. My feeling is that too much television takes people away from interacting with one another, that it is a subtle but constant propaganda machine for the establishment, that it does tend to glorify violence as a mode of behavior, that it encourages passivity. I feel that a certain amount of limitation of the time a child watches television and the kind of program he watches, especially during the early years, is helpful to a child's development. I do feel that the substitution of too much television for a child's fantasy life may have a limiting effect on the development of his creative potential. I do not believe that watching violence will necessarily tend to result in a child's becoming violent, but I do feel it might influence his taking belligerent warlike positions on issues rather than peaceful ones that involve mediation. All in all I think it is very likely that studies in the future will show very severe damage done to children by television. It may ultimately be listed as an addiction along with smoking, marijuana, food, drugs, and alcohol.

I do think that as a parent you should try to define some of your own views and positions on these issues, and then you should impart them to your children in a way that invades their rights and individuality as little as possible. However, I do not think you should handle the issue by not handling—by abdicating your responsibility. Television is a very cheap baby-sitter. It also gets you off the hook of having to relate to your children. It is very seductive to accept it as a fact of life about which you have no choice for your children. But just as you can influence their choice of friends, and should because they incorporate pieces of their behavior, you should influence their watching television since they are also incorporating pieces of the Wolf-Man, the Boston Strangler, Hitler, and quite a few other unsavory people whom you would not wittingly invite into your home. On the positive side there are many educational programs for children that are genuinely helpful and enlightening for them. You can help decide whether you will invite Sesame Street or Jack the Ripper into your home.

It seems to me that in general the younger the child the more you should restrict the television programs he watches. Even infants and babies are exposed to television today. You must remember that their emotional systems cannot handle the noise and excitement of a shoot-em-up western. Probably during the first and second years of life it would be better not to expose a child to television at all. You cannot predict the nature of the commercials, and they might be very frightening to an infant or baby (in some ways, some of them frighten me!). After two, a very careful selection of children's programs and nature films might be appropriate. Cartoon programs have to be chosen very carefully. Some of them are filled with violence and are hardly fare for two or three year olds. After four, cartoons are probably all right or at least unavoidable. Of course if there are older children in the house, especially with only one television set, admittedly you are going to have a problem. Many homes now have two or more sets and that helps. You will have to work hard to effect it, but it may be worth your while to keep careful control in television watching. The problem is compounded because the effects, though far-reaching, may be very subtle and not able to be proven till years later. I would definitely keep young children—certainly under ten—away from news programs with their reports of war and crime, many films, certainly including horror films and many westerns and crime-type serials. After ten, it will probably be a losing battle to try to exert much influence, though you may still prohibit certain especially lurid crime programs. The important thing is for you not to abdicate your role. Make some choices and decisions and do your best to effect them. Remember that you are in charge.

SIBLING RIVALRY

Sibling rivalry, that is, jealousy between your children, is a fact of life and it has to be faced. Both for your own sake and that of the children it is desirable to reduce it. One of the ways of trying to lessen it is to prepare a child carefully for the arrival of a new baby. It is no easy matter for a child to have a rival sprung on him that is younger, cuter, demands more care and is the focus of everyone's interest, attention and adulation. The more preparation there is for the event, and the more the parents try consciously to give the older child his share of attention at the time of the arrival of the new baby, the less severe the trauma will be.

Explanations about the arrival of the new baby will probably fall on deaf ears when the older sibling is under two. Nevertheless it is still a good idea to tell the child that a new baby is coming, to get a doll and put it in a crib, to let the older sibling feel your belly. It is also important not to have any major changes right around the time of the newborn's return from the hospital. If the older sibling is going to change rooms, the move should occur several weeks before the birth. Also it is very important for the child to get used to the person who is going to take care of him and to have her around the house for a couple of weeks before the delivery. For older children after three and a half, more extensive explanations should be attempted and will be understood by some and more and more as the child is older. A four year old may not grasp the whole concept of birth too well, but a six or seven year old very likely will. The older child should not be sent to nursery school around the time of the birth or it will be experienced as a banishment; it should be done several weeks before the delivery. These preparations and explanations are extremely important in reducing the trauma of the event.

Strangely enough my own earliest memory was at age two when my sister was born. I was sent away from my city home (*not* a good idea) to strange surroundings on a farm with a whole group of relatives, no one of whom I knew well (*not* a good idea) and no specific one of whom was designated as a mother surrogate. I remember crawling under a table while they were eating. I felt totally lost and displaced. I had no idea what was happening or why my life had suddenly been disrupted. I remember feeling very sad and totally despairing and having no idea what the future held for me. Of course, my parents had done everything exactly wrong. But this experience left me with an understanding of how disruptive being displaced by another child can be.

When the mother comes home from the hospital, it is wise for her to try to play down her enthusiasm for the new baby in the older siblings' presence and to take care of the new baby as much as is possible, especially breast feeding, out of the sight of the siblings. It is also wise to pay as much attention to the older siblings as possible. If the older sibling or siblings regress and want to drink from a bottle or be held more or even temporarily break their toilet training, it is wise to try to go along with this without any fuss. They may even want to breast feed, but they should not be allowed to do this. It is also a good idea to acknowledge the jealousy openly and with humor. I remember the pleasure and relief on my five-year-old daughter's face when I could joke with her about her wanting to throw the baby down the incinerator or throw him out of the window to see if he would bounce. This handling of the situation with humor faces the jealousy head on, but makes it seem natural rather than grim and sadistic; it obviously reduces the guilt about it.

The pretense that many parents try to keep up that they like each child the same amount at every stage of their development is apt to confuse a child because you will be saying one thing and expressing another in your feeling responses. I think it is straighter and more honest for a parent to acknowledge to himself that he is more drawn toward one child than to another at any particular point in time. He does not have to go out of his way to tell the other child or children this, but neither does he have to deny it when he is asked about it or confronted with it as a reality. I remember my favorite child switching back and forth several times depending on their particular age and the degree of my involvement with them. The children will know anyway which one is favored. Being able to live with *not* being the favorite is something we must get used to in life. It is a challenge and it can have positive results. Of course, if one child is consistently and constantly the favorite of both parents, it can make life difficult not only for the other children but for that child himself. I have many patients who felt so guilty about surpassing their siblings in the parents' favor or in other areas that they actually were inhibited about succeeding or enjoying life too much. And, of course, the "unfavorite" may harbor a great deal of anger and hurt.

Children are usually too diplomatic to ask directly "Which of us do you like better?" If they do, no matter at what age, it is advisable to be honest, especially if you can say truthfully, "Well, right now I like Joe better. But when you were smaller there were times I liked you better and maybe after a while I'll like you better again. It's that way for all parents and children." You can acknowledge it must feel bad not to be the favorite without apologizing for your feelings. If you like or favor girls over boys or vice versa, you can admit it openly also. This is part of a total approach of being honest about your feelings rather than telling your children what you think will be "good" for them or what they want to hear. It helps them to verify their perceptions of reality (they *know* they aren't favored

at that time) rather than confusing them and leaving them
to feel that their perceptions are incorrect. So many of my
patients became patients because their parents under-
mined these kinds of perceptions by lying to them "for
their own good." Besides it helps children to confront a
reality that is not always the way they would want it to
be. When they grow up, they may not be the boss's favorite either. Learning to live with unpleasant realities as
children paves the way for being able to let go, being
separate and independent and being able later in life to
cope with reality.

Many of my patients developed serious problems because they had siblings who either died or were physically
or emotionally ill or were retarded or deformed. These
"defective" children usually commanded the lion's share
of the parents' attention. The healthy sibling is in a terrible bind between feeling furious at the sick one for getting
the parents' attention and feeling compassion for the sick
child's disability. The rage they feel toward the sick child
is unacceptable to them, and they usually direct it against
themselves and develop some kind of self-destructive
patterns. These situations of a sick or defective child in a
home with healthy siblings are so loaded with difficult
emotional tensions that they usually require some kind of
professional investigation and guidance. Of course, they
cause untold suffering and conflicts and guilts in parents
as well as siblings.

As a matter of fact when there is very serious hostility
between normal siblings, the situation usually bears looking into. A certain amount of teasing and bickering and
fighting over the "best" seat at the table or in the car or
the biggest piece of cake is within normal limits, especially
if it is open and can be dealt with in a humorous way. But
if the rivalry loses its humor and becomes bitter, grim,
consistent, or is expressed in physical or verbal sadism
that creates an acutely tense atmosphere, then it is time to
take stock and do something about it either by yourself
starting with an open, communicative discussion of it, or
—that failing—with some professional help.

At the bottom of most serious sibling rivalry lies some

form of parental deprivation. Most children who get "good enough" mothering are not going to be *that* rivalrous with their siblings. The cases of a sick child in the family might well be exceptions to this, but even there the degree of trauma is directly proportional to the quality of the mothering. As far as treating children alike, you cannot help *feeling* a preference toward one or the other at any particular time, but you certainly can try to *behave* in a way that is *fair* to all and does not openly discriminate against one or more. If you get one of them a candy bar, the others should be offered the same privilege. If one goes to camp at a certain age, the others, if it is possible, should also be given the choice of going. If this is not possible—say because of a financial reverse—it should be explained carefully. If one gets something one day, the other or others should be assured they will get their turn at the appropriate time when the opportunity presents itself.

In this area you as a person and a parent are entitled to feel whatever you feel. This is another instance of not only allowing yourself to be an authentic parent, but of allowing it because it is right. You do not have to feel guilty for liking one child more than the other. Attempting to deny this either to yourself or to your children or trying to overcompensate to balance things just causes confusion. You will be double binding your children by saying one thing and then expressing other feelings nonverbally. You can acknowledge your preferences and at the same time try in your behavior to be fair and not discriminate.

If a child does feel jealous, it is a good thing to let him express his jealousy openly and even consciously to encourage such expressions. The expressions, of course, must be limited to words. The other child, especially if he is younger, must be protected against the older child's wrath. Often the acceptance of the feeling of hatred toward the other child acts to diminish the guilt feelings about it, and also tends to limit some of the acting out.

One of the most destructive devices we can use to control a child's behavior is to produce guilt in the child. I am sure that all of us, including unfortunately myself, have used this method on occasion. It is destructive but effective in the short run in getting children to do what we want them to do, so most of us are tempted to use it. It is another form of dirty pool, however, because we simultaneously create hostility and disarm the child so he cannot find an appropriate way of discharging the hostility. The classic guilt binds include "You'll give me a heart attack," "I'll die and then you'll be sorry," "You only have one mother; you should try to make her happy," "If you do that, I'll kill myself." Sam Levenson has a classic joke, indicating the universality of this method of dealing with children: "My mother was always threatening to kill herself by jumping out the window, but we kids didn't worry too much about it since we lived in a basement apartment."

Some of the grosser, cruder ways of binding by guilt have become legendary and the subjects of jokes. So now more sophisticated parents are not apt to use them. However, more subtle variations spring up to replace them and are not as distinguishable to parents or child as their predecessors. (An example would be: "You can do it, but I'll worry." Another favorite: "It's all right with me, but your father [mother] will be very upset.")

Another method of binding by guilt is to keep telling your child how many sacrifices you are making for him. I have a patient who remembers with dread his father repeatedly telling him how much it cost him to send him to private school. Others rub in how the child gets the best food or clothing or sleeping accommodations while the parents deprive themselves. Now there are certainly times when it may be very appropriate—and feels good rather than self-denying—for a parent to sacrifice some of his own pleasures and comforts for a child. But if you do this, get your reward from the act itself. Don't try to elicit sympathy or credit or gratitude from your child. If you *don't* ask for gratitude, you will probably get it. If you do ask for it, you will probably arouse hostility (at least unconsciously) from your child. You will also bind your child by producing guilt. Please, no more, "After all I've done for you . . ."

What makes this method of controlling much worse than others is that since you are professing your hurt or sacrifice or the imminence of physical damage to yourself, the child does not feel free to fight you or even to entertain hostile thoughts or fantasies toward you. Even the most authoritarian methods of control are not as destructive as controlling through guilt. In such authoritarian situations, even in sadistic ones, at least the victim can feel free to hate his oppressor. With control by guilt, the anger generated in the child has no place to go except back against the self. This can result in depression, self-hatred, masochistic behavior, psychosomatic problems or other self-destructive symptoms.

Aside from controlling a child in this way, using guilt also tends to bind a child to you. You are holding him very very close—in the wrong way and at the wrong time, and you are making it harder for him to let go. You burden him with the responsibility for your safety, happiness, health and even life. He will not dare to leave you for fear you will not be able to survive without him. So this impedes the process of separation. I often say that we psychoanalysts should build a monument to this kind of parent. Without such parents we would practically be out of business.

The harsh-sounding but valid conclusion is that it is better even to beat a child than it is to use guilt as a way of binding and controlling him. This is one type of parental behavior you should really try to avoid.

RELIGION

How to handle religion with the children is obviously a very individual matter. Again, it is basically a question of your own *authentic* beliefs. Some people espouse the idea that even though they do not believe in any religion themselves, they "owe it" to their children to expose them to a branch of organized religion. This idea makes little sense to me. The adoption of a religious belief in today's times is almost always through identification with parents. Of course, there are exceptions to this broad generalization, but it is basically true. I doubt that exposure to organized religion by parents who are non-believers results very often in the children adopting the religion in a sincere way. The pressure on the children to spend time learning about something their parents do not really believe in often produces a good deal of hostility toward the parents. Many of my patients recall with great resentment the hours they spent in religious instruction.

Of course if you are a serious believer, you don't have a problem. You will and should try to impose your beliefs on your children. If you have a good relationship with them and they identify positively with you, there is a good chance that they will follow your religious example because they have reason in the rest of their relationship with you to trust and respect you. Of course other influences may come into their lives that may cause them to change their religious beliefs. It seems to me that this rule should apply to "devout" atheists and agnostics as well as to devout observers. If you believe in *not* believing, this is something too that can and should be communicated to your children.

The problems arise more in situations in which the parents are actually not sincere believers but merely go through the most superficial motions on the rarest occasions. This creates another double bind for children. You are telling them to do as I say, not as I do or feel. They are confused. It seems unfair for them to go through the trouble of learning all kinds of rote and dogma when you obviously do not believe in it or follow it yourself. If you are one of those who has just a nominal relationship to a particular religion but basically do not believe in it or practice it, I think it would be wise for you to try to put yourself in the position of your child to see if you can experience the kind of confusion you may be causing him.

It is still your decision to make, and you have the right to impose your way. If you impose on your child a system you do not follow or believe in, you might at least consider the possibility of giving him a long, clear explanation of the reasons for your doing it.

When two parents have different religions, they often have as part of their marriage ceremony an agreement as to which religion the children will follow. If parents do not have such a formalized agreement, then they should certainly make this decision themselves. It is highly inappropriate to give children under twelve the choice of what religion *they* should follow. Even with the agreement, though, there is no reason why each parent should not feel free to be his authentic self and respond to the children's questions about what his personal beliefs may be. Naturally this should not be done in a manner that subtly sabotages or subverts the previous agreement. But there is no reason why parents should have to pretend to be united in this or any other issue, since by definition that would reduce the ability of both of them to be real and authentic.

During the past few years there has been a tendency for young people to become very much immersed in religious movements from Billy Graham to the "Jesus Freaks" to some of the Eastern religious denominations like Buddhism. Whether you applaud or deplore this is very much a matter of your individual point of view. Even though it is usually people in middle or late adolescence who follow these leaders and your power and influence over your children may have diminished considerably at that point, it is still worthwhile for you to make your own position quite clear, especially if it is a negative position. If you have had a good relationship with your child, you may still be able to prevent him from going in a direction that is not to your liking. Don't assume that he is old enough to know his own mind or that religion is personal and you have no right to interfere. Let him know where you stand. Then, even if he goes against your wishes, at least he will have achieved some of the psychological benefits of "letting go."

The English psychoanalyst, Bowlby, has an entire volume describing the effects of separations from parents on infants and young children. Without going into great detail, prolonged separation from a parent during the first year of life starts out by producing a profound terror—one that makes a horror movie look like a picnic. Looking at it from the infant's point of view, what he experiences is the loss (very likely forever in his mind) of what he perceives to be his only nurturing source. He expects to be abandoned and left to starve. It is somewhat analogous to what you would feel like if you were left on a desert island that had no vegetation on it. Toward the latter part of the first year the baby begins to have the capacity to internalize his image of the mother so that when she is out of sight he still carries around her image which gives him some security about her returning to him. Following the terror of too early or too prolonged separation during infancy the baby goes into a feeling of despair, depression and hopelessness. Then he cuts off his feelings, and goes into a kind of withdrawal from the world. If this sequence is repeated often enough, the child will be very fearful of separations from loved ones in his adult life and have very strong reactions to this. If it is repeated very frequently or there is no steady significant figure around during much of his first year of life, the child will withdraw his feelings in a more permanent way from the external world and never be able to get close to or involved with another human being.

It is for this reason that I feel that the fewer separations from mother during the first and second years the better off the child will be. By this I mean overnight separations or longer ones. Hold them very close! Naturally separations for matters of hours are unavoidable and may be even helpful to growth. However, when a mother leaves a child, she should tell the child she is leaving and if at all possible leave the child with a familiar figure—father, steady baby-sitter, grandmother, maid or relative. My own personal preference would be for the parents not even to go away from the child for a week-end trip during the first two years. To compound the problem, I feel that bringing a child on an extended trip that lasts several days of travel time during the first two years is also extremely traumatic for him. During this period he requires the security of a stable environment as well as a stable relationship with a significant figure. Moving should also be avoided if there is any choice. I feel that the parents are really quite bound to their child during the first two years of his life. After that they can begin to leave—at first for short periods and then for gradually lengthening ones. But during these periods there should be someone around that the child knows and trusts.

If a mother falls ill and has to be hospitalized or otherwise must be absent during the first two years, a great deal of attention should be paid to the child's reaction. The father should be as omnipresent as possible and other significant figures such as maids, grandparents or other relatives should be on hand to ease what will nonetheless be a very significant traumatic experience. If there is any way to avoid the separation, such as bringing the child to the hospital to be with the mother, frequent telephone contact if the child is old enough, or in other situations if the mother has any other options open to her other than leaving her child, they should have the highest kind of priority. As I have said before, I think the ideal situation for a child is probably the one the Indians use of keeping the child strapped to the mother. Now I am aware that I am disagreeing with the point of view of many feminists who feel that the woman's development in other areas should not be cut off for two whole years. I am also disagreeing with the idea of day-care centers for children under two, with Bruno Bettelheim's feelings that children can be brought up in a kibbutz with shared mothering. I am sure further studies will clarify which views are correct. However, at this moment, my own readings, experiences and personal observations of myself, my family, my friends, and my patients lead me to feel quite strongly that lengthy separations between mother and the child under two can have profound deleterious effects.

Almost the reverse is true of separations at later ages, from about six years of age upward. Meals, and later sleepovers at houses of friends, overnight visits with grandparents and other relatives, should be encouraged. Baby-sitters can be introduced and used with increasing frequency. As the child grows older, different baby-sitters can be used. These can bring about a furthering of self-hood providing the child is left in a stable environment with a secure, significant figure. Between two and six there can be a gradual but cautious increase in the periods of separation. At a later age even the swapping of children between families for periods of a month can provide increased growth. Of course, many children will go away to camp for as long as two months at ages eight or nine, and this can well turn out to be a period of emotional growth and furthering of independence. Few children are ready for such an experience before the age of eight. Being in a new environment without any familiar figures around them is likely to prove to be very traumatic to younger children.

Talking about separations from parents, one of the absolutely most terrifying experiences for a child under eight is to be in a hospital either for a sickness or—even worse—for an operation without having his mother there with him. One can only imagine the absolute terror at such an experience seen through a child's eyes. Several of my patients entered such situations in their childhood much to their detriment. I would absolutely never allow any child under eight to be in a hospital that did not provide facilities for his mother to be at his side through this horrendous experience. I think any responsible parent should do his utmost to be with his hospitalized child, though he might have to brook a great deal of opposition from many hospitals.

In order to get the flavor of what a separation during the first two years of life feels like, you should try to put yourself in the position of the child and try to experience the world as he does. If you can do this, you will be able to judge how much separation your particular child will be able to tolerate without serious consequences at any particular point in time.

Now suppose that while reading this you suddenly realize to your horror that you had your baby delivered in a hospital that only allowed you to see him every four hours, that you went back to work when the baby was three months old and left him with a number of different nursemaids, seeing little of him yourself, that you and your husband went off to Europe for two weeks when he was a year old, and so on. What can you do now that your child is eight years old? Should you give up your job and stay home with him all day long? The answer is, of course, *absolutely not.* You cannot make up now for what happened then. *Then* he needed to be held very close. *Now* he needs to be let go. Holding the child close now would only compound the problem. If your child seems relatively happy now, perhaps, after all, you made up for some of the lack of *quantity* closeness by the *quality* closeness you gave him. Or perhaps some of the others around him did. You cannot reverse or change the past. Do the best thing for your child at his present age level; the best thing is of course what is appropriate for that age, not what might have been appropriate at one year of age. You did the best you could with the knowledge you had available to you then.

SANTA CLAUS, THE EASTER BUNNY, AND OTHER MYTHS

Though in general, and in almost every instance, I think it is extremely important for a parent to be totally honest with his child, never to lie to him or deceive him, I think an exception to this has to be made as far as Santa Claus, the Easter Bunny, the Tooth Fairy and other such fantasy figures are concerned. These fantasies are so harmless and bring so much joy to children that it seems a shame to deprive them of these pleasures. I can say that I have never seen an erosion in the trust a child feels toward a parent because of the deception around these particular figures. It almost seems as if the child understands the necessity of the deception and feels that it is really in his own interest, so that he never holds this against his parents or trusts them less because of this particular lack of truthfulness. I would not tell my child that there is no Santa Claus until, usually at age six, he realizes it clearly himself and at that point any further lies would be pointless.

—————————DEATH OR SEVERE ILLNESS IN THE FAMILY

I believe that, just as in the case of sex, any questions a child asks about death or illness should be answered as fully, truthfully and directly as befits his capacity to understand, at his age level. By the time the child is three, he should have a fairly good idea what death is all about. He will have seen animals, birds, and pets die and will ask questions about this. Pets incidentally are often very helpful to children. They can relate to animals very intensely, but, of course, not as intensely as they do to people. They can experience all kinds of emotions in relationship to them including the feelings of mourning and loss that come about with the death of a loved one. In this way they can become accustomed to dealing with specific sets of feelings, becoming desensitized and immunized, so to speak, in order to deal with similar situations in relationship to people. Now I am not trying to boil down a child's relationship to a pet to a bunch of psychological jargon. It is a very real relationship that has a validity in its own right regardless of any psychological advantages. I am merely stating that as an added plus there are these psychological advantages. And a very important one has to do with being helpful in explaining death as well as illness, birth, sex, mothering, reaction to loss, sibling rivalry and many other situations in animals that parallel human situations. The famous stories about explaining sex to a child using "the birds and the bees" is a common example of this. Of course the jokes about this show the parent getting so far off human sexuality when describing sex in the birds and the bees that his explanations become ludicrous. We must be careful that our explanations of sex do not become equally so. This also applies to explanations about death. It is best to try to keep philosophical and religious issues to a minimum and give the child a straightforward explanation that he can understand. He is not apt to be able to refer to Kant or Nietzsche or Saint Thomas Aquinas to get documentation of a complicated explanation.

If there is a death in the family, it seems to me that from age three on the child should be included in the whole process of the funeral if the person who dies had a meaningful relationship to the child. Excluding the child from this on the basis of protecting him is, in my opinion, unwise. It does him a great disservice and leaves him with all sorts of doubts and imaginings about what may have happened and why it happened. When I was seven years old, my sister, age five, died. Aside from being told very perfunctorily that she had died and that it was from an operation on her ear, I did not receive any explanation. No one asked me about my feelings about her or her death. There was no opportunity to ventilate my grief, my feelings of loss, my pleasure in disposing of a hated rival, or anything else. This event perhaps more than any other one in my life resulted in untold emotional suffering for me—not only at the time of her death but with continuing effect throughout my life. Not to use you, the reader, as a captive audience for a confessional, but to give you an idea of the long-term effects of the mishandling of such a situation, I will tell you some of the details of my particular story. I remember well that I did not really believe the story about the ear operation, but I had a strong fantasy that some bad men had stolen into the house, kidnapped her, and killed her. Aside from remembering this fantasy, I repressed almost all reactions to her death. It was only years and years later that these emotions were elicited again as part of a psychoanalytic process that helped me reconstruct them. As a matter of fact the emotions were so deeply buried that all ordinary psychoanalytic techniques failed to uncover them. I ultimately had to visit the grave of my sister accompanied by my analyst decades after her actual death before the totality of my emotional reactions could be unearthed. Now I am sure that my parents were well meaning and wished to protect me from unpleasantness, but in fact their not handling this situation correctly cost me an enormous amount of suffering during my life. I also do not by any means imply that *all* of this suffering was specifically connected with my sister's death and the manner in which my parents dealt with it. Obviously there had to be and there were many other variables in the picture including a grossly pathological family interaction. However, some of the problems I shall elucidate appear to have a rather direct connection with her death and their response to it.

One of my problems involved the choice of female companions. I had a strong tendency to pick women who were quite ill psychologically and to put a tremendous effort into trying to rehabilitate them. This appeared to be an attempt to expiate the guilt I felt over the unconscious desire to get my sister out of the way because she represented a hated sibling rival. By bringing back to life women who were lost souls I was attempting to undo the guilt I felt and the responsibility I took for "killing" my sister. My sister was in fact a tremendously charismatic child who was the darling of everyone. She became sanctified in the family after her death, which increased my rivalrous feelings as well as my guilt. But the hostility and guilt were only one aspect of my feelings. I also truly loved my sister and felt extremely close to her, closer in fact than I felt toward any other member of my family. We had a very warm relationship; she was my best friend, trusted confidante and adviser, and her beauty and loveliness and charisma enchanted me as well as other family members. Her death was to me a tremendous loss. I did not remember my grief, but experienced it in analysis years later. Her loss was such a devastating blow to me that on some level I resolved never to allow myself to care that much for another person and be that totally committed to her, because I did not want to experience the same pain lest I should lose the person through death or some other means. This unconscious mechanism to protect myself against the possibility of reexperiencing the pain kept me from making a total commitment to another person until it had been worked out analytically. Other side effects were a tremendous sensitivity to abandonment that forced me to choose people who were very dependent on me and therefore could never have the option of leaving me. Of course, there were all kinds of other ramifications and manifestations that could directly or indirectly be attributable to this traumatic event.

In the course of my practice I have had many many patients, some of whose problems appeared to be attributable directly or indirectly, wholly or in part to deaths in the family during their childhood. If such a misfortune should occur, the handling of it with a child requires tremendous skill and understanding. If you feel you cannot be sure of your ability to do so optimally, it might be well to get advice from a trusted friend or a professional. The long-term consequences, as you can see, may be enormous.

The way that death is presented to a child should be clear and simple and concise. If a death in the immediate family occurs before the child is three, it might be appropriate to say, "Grandma is dead. That means that she will not be here with us ever again. Do you understand what I mean? Is there anything you want to know about it? If you have some feelings about this either now or later, try to tell me about them." When the child is between three and five, a fuller explanation might be in order. "Grandma has died. Do you know what that means? It's the same as what happened to your turtle. She stopped breathing and being alive and will not be with us any more. We are going to bring her to a place called a cemetery where we will bury her. I would like you to come along with us when we do this. They will put her body in a box and put her in the ground and then cover her with earth. Then we will never see her. I feel very badly about her dying. I loved her a lot and I will miss her. Do you have any feelings about not seeing Grandma again?" Then, of course, I would answer any questions in a straightforward manner.

And obviously I would try to include the child in at least some parts of the funeral process. At this age I would tend to leave religious aspects out of it because they would merely be confusing to a child. "Grandma is up in heaven with God" is beyond a five year old's capacity to understand.

After the child has reached age five, I would merely elaborate on the above, including some of the medical data about death coming from illness or accident or old age and alleviating any anxiety the child might have about these issues. From six or seven on if you have strong religious beliefs that have to do with sincerely believing that Grandma is up in heaven with God, perhaps at this age your child might begin to understand it, but with difficulty. From this age on you could also explain some of people's reactions to death, including mourning and some of the religious and cultural rituals that accompany death. I feel it is most appropriate not to hide your own grief from a child of any age. He may not fully understand it, especially if he is under two or three, but he will see you to be an authentic person and may later on in his life connect your emotional reaction to the death. Showing children real feeling (unless it is sadism) can never really harm them. It presents them with a picture of the real world through your being real. It gives them a good model for the expression of feelings rather than their suppression, and it eventually helps them let go of you because they see you as separate and different from them with your own set of feelings which do not necessarily parallel theirs.

The same advice applies to a serious illness in a member of the family. After age three I see no reason for a child to be lied to and protected against what is going on. He will realize anyway that something serious is happening. It will relieve rather than increase his anxiety to have it named and specified. It will also prepare him in case of the death of the person, so that shock will not be total and sudden. It is much easier to deal with a death after an illness than with a sudden death, say from an accident. Why not allow the child to be in on it as you the adult are?

Recently a friend of ours had a child, age eleven, who developed an inoperable brain tumor. Without going into grisly detail, I advised her to tell the other children, ages seven and thirteen, that their brother was seriously ill. We have another friend who recently had a mastectomy and tried to hide the whole thing from her seven-year-old daughter. I felt this was a serious mistake. Not knowing *what* is going on but knowing something serious is going on produces a great deal more anxiety than knowing exactly what is happening. It is like comparing walking across a field toward an enemy in a *High Noon* type showdown with walking across a field where there are snipers hidden in the bushes. Once again, being real, being yourself is what turns out to be best for you and your child. Besides, the child might find out from some outside source and this might be a sudden shock, or the outside source might not tell the news in a reassuring, explanatory way. Suppose a friend suddenly tells your child, "Your brother is dying of a brain tumor," or "Your mother has cancer."

MOVING AND CHANGING SCHOOLS

Moving to a different home and changing schools is obviously not always a matter of choice. I do not want to frighten you into thinking that, if you are forced to move, your child will be a psychological basket-case for life. However it is important to know what some of the consequences of moving are for a child. This may influence your decision if you do have some choice in the matter or may help you handle some of your child's anxieties and insecurities if you must move at a particular time.

Let me start off by reporting some of the memories a patient of mine told me about her constantly shifting homes and schools and some of the effects this appeared to have had on her. Again this patient came from a very disturbed family and the consequences and reactions to her moves did not stem from the moving alone. Her father was an Army officer who shifted from post to post in her earliest years. Subsequently he became ill and was shifted from one Army hospital to another. This occurred during much of her elementary and secondary school life. During this period she was not in Army posts but had to live in towns near the Army hospitals and attend numerous unfamiliar schools. Sometimes she would be shifted in the middle of a semester, depending on the whims of the Army orders. She recalls never feeling she belonged anywhere. When she entered a new class in a new school, she would be the "foreigner" or "stranger." Often the other children would have some particular skill or knowledge that she did not possess. In their characteristically sadistic way the other children would poke fun at her and continually humiliate her. She also dressed and spoke somewhat differently from them, and she was an object of ridicule on this account. Children form strong in-group feelings, and she was usually excluded from such inner circles for a considerable length of time after her arrival. Often when she had finally achieved a sense of being in and knowing the ground rules of what was acceptable behavior in that particular club and also had begun to get the hang of what was to be known academically and what ways it was to be presented to this particular teacher, she was abruptly transferred to another new school. This patient, an extremely attractive, intelligent and successful professional as well as a wife and mother, never feels at home in any new situation. She always expects to be rejected by new neighbors, friends, professional colleagues. She finds it difficult to shop in department stores and expects to be humiliated by the clerks as not belonging there. She always has the feeling she is not dressed properly for whatever the occasion may be. She has difficulty feeling that she is accepted by her co-workers and even by her maid. These particular problems appear to bear a direct relationship to her childhood experiences of having to move and having to try to adjust to new schools and playmates constantly and repeatedly.

Now again I want to emphasize that this patient's family background was otherwise disturbed and that she was certainly exposed to an inordinate amount of moving in her childhood. One move for a child that comes from a stable family is certainly not apt to produce this. However, even one move can cause quite a disruption especially in the life of a younger child. As a generality, the younger the child, the more traumatic the dislocation. When this occurs, it is advisable to spend more time with the child, helping him ventilate his feelings and showing understanding about what may well be a difficult academic and social adjustment. It might be wise to help him form peer relationships through contact with other parents and through inviting neighborhood children over and helping make introductions to peers who might not be particularly welcoming to the child.

CHILDREN'S FEARS

In the course of development children often exhibit a number of specific fears. Some of the more common ones are fears of the dark, thunder and lightning, loud noises, dogs, cats, snakes, other animals, school, going to a strange bathroom, certain unfamiliar people—especially older people—ghosts, movie or television monsters, fire, things under their beds or lurking in their bedrooms. The important thing to remember about these fears is that they represent *phobic* formations. The fears are not really of what they seem to be but are symbolic representations of some inner conflict, very often some difficulty in the parent-child relationship. These phobic formations are not uncommon and frequently can appear in connection with some particular traumatic event in the house or out of it. If they are relatively transitory and infrequent, they probably do not require professional help. They may be dealt with through reassurance or, if you happen to be a particularly psychologically sophisticated parent, with an attempt to figure out what particular event brought on this particular phobia. It is important to understand that phobias are beyond a child's control, that he does not develop a phobia as an interpersonal maneuver to give you a hard time or otherwise thwart you. Childhood fears come about as an unconscious process and, if they persist, they can usually be unraveled by a skillful psychotherapist. Freud wrote a famous case report on the analysis of a fear of horses in a five-year-old child, little Hans. This phobia was traced to be determined by an unconscious fear that his father would castrate him and that his mother would have another baby. The formation of a phobia is a complicated process, that would require a long explanation. But, in short, fear of the dark means a great deal more to a child than a fear of the dark. He cannot help developing it, and he cannot turn it off by willpower. Sometimes reassurance and sympathetic understanding will help it go away; sometimes they will not. If a fear persists, it is time to consider obtaining professional help. The phobic symptom is just the tip of the iceberg. There is something else going on underneath that you will probably not be able to fathom.

THE RAPPROCHEMENT PERIOD: TRANSITIONAL OBJECTS, SECURITY BLANKETS

"Transitional objects" is simply fancy psychoanalysts' language to describe security blankets, teddy bears, pillows, rags or other objects that children carry around with them as a source of security. Though most parents can identify this much about them, I feel there are a few other facts that might be helpful to know and understand. Transitional objects have a very important role in the "letting go" process. Children have the difficult task of going from the state of being totally merged with their mothers to being separate, independent people. These objects represent a stand-in or substitute for the mother while the separation from her is being accomplished. So their use should not be discouraged even if it continues as late as age ten. Usually they are given up around the age of four or five. This separation process begins at the end of the first year of life and, when things go well, is quite advanced by the end of the third year. In going from being tied to mother to being free from her there is naturally a period of considerable anxiety as the tie is broken and the child experiences himself as free. This freedom brings a sense of adventure and creativity, but it also brings some sense of panic. Transitional objects help to relieve that anxiety.

Another of the ways children have of dealing with this panic is to run back to mother for "refueling." As a matter of fact, this phenomenon begins rather regularly during the latter part of the second year of life and, theoretically, should be accomplished by the end of the third year. However, my own experience is that most of us never totally negotiate this process successfully. With every move toward a more autonomous independent position, we usually require support and reassurance.

The child's motor and cognitive (intellectual) development push him farther and farther away from mother toward exploring his own interests. Suddenly he finds himself out there all alone. He is frightened and runs back to cling to mother. This running back is called the "rapprochement" phase of the separation-individuation process. How the mother handles this period is very crucial to the child's development and his ability to let go. If the mother has been relieved that the child is finally letting go of her, she may see this return as a regression to a state she was beginning to think had passed. So she may be rejecting and punitive rather than supportive of this move back to her, which is only a temporary measure. This will frighten the child and make him move back to merging with her, instead of just briefly seeking her comfort and support. On the other hand, if she consciously or unconsciously wants to hold the child close to her and never let him go, she can jump at this opportunity and feel that the child was not ready to be turned loose in the first place. Instead of giving a temporary refueling, she can use this opportunity to bind him and to subvert his efforts at independence. This is a pretty ticklish period that requires great sensitivity on the part of the mother. She has to reassure the child that she is available in case of need but also continue to encourage the child's explorations and wanderings away from her.

The way you deal with bad language is very much a function of your own subjective reaction to it. On one end of the spectrum will be those of you who feel that even a "damn" is immoral and totally inappropriate coming from a child's or maybe even an adult's mouth. On the other end there are parents who feel any curse words or four-letter words are part of all people's modes of expression, even children's, a form of communication they find totally unobjectionable in their home. Even these parents, however, will be impelled to point out to their children under what circumstances this language is appropriate and under what circumstances it is not. Otherwise their children will quickly get themselves into all sorts of trouble with police, teachers, principals, ministers, and so on.

Children of three and four seem to get a delight out of using anal words, such as "doody," "booger," "pee pee," and the like. This is certainly a harmless expression of a continuing interest in bowel and bladder functions that has had to be modified during toilet training. It usually passes by age six. However, if these expressions are *especially* offensive to you, there is no need to hide that fact. But don't be too disappointed if you are not able completely to extinguish this kind of language at this age without resort to the sort of punishment that might well be more damaging.

Depending upon the neighborhood the child lives in and his companions, he is quite likely to begin to hear four-letter words at about the age of six. Using them will be a way of connecting with his peers and, if the parents object, forming a bond with those peers that in fact aids in his separation—his letting go—from his parents. It certainly does not necessarily have to represent a dreadful habit that bodes ill for his future or his morality.

However, the choice of whether to allow, encourage or totally forbid the use of such language in your presence must be yours. If you object, you should make this objection clear and concrete and punish any violations. Do not allow it one day and then object to it the next. Also, if you yourself curse like a trooper at home, but do not allow the children to do so, this will put a strain on them. However, it is possible for you to enforce even this system. You can say that cursing is a privilege allowed only to grown-ups in this house. In any event, take your stand, whatever it may be: be real and authentic about enforcing it.

THE ONLY CHILD

Many parents say that they decided to have another child because it is not good for a child not to have a brother or sister. I do not know of any evidence to support the idea that emotional problems and difficulties are more common among only children. In my own practice I cannot say that there has been a preponderance of only children or even a disproportionately large number of them. If having siblings is a big factor in increasing mental health, this fact seems to have eluded me and any colleagues of my acquaintance.

It would seem that a child who does not have siblings might have a harder time separating emotionally from his mother. I suppose this might be true up to a certain point. Joining with a sibling—or a father—is a step in the process of breaking away from mother. However, this is only one of so many variables that it does not appear to have a major effect. One might also imagine that an only child strangely enough might have more problems dealing with rivalry than one who has had siblings. This might be attributed to his not being forced by reality to deal with these issues. Here too getting "good enough" mothering versus suffering maternal deprivation seems to carry more weight in producing difficulties than of being an only child. One might think the parents of only children would be more apt to be overprotective, but here again this is probably brought about more by emotional difficulties in the parents than it is by the circumstance of their having but one child. One might also speculate that an only child would be more prone to loneliness and to becoming an introvert; this too seems to be determined more by other factors.

In sum, there is no strong evidence that you are doing your child a major disservice by not providing him with siblings. Sometimes the reverse may obviously be true. I remember one of my patients reporting to me that her older brother was chiding her about her emotional problems. He came from the same family, he said. How come he was such a model of mental health whereas she was so neurotic? I suggested she tell him the reason was that he did not have an older brother like himself around during his childhood.

The important issue in all this for most parents is that they should decide on the basis of *their* own wishes whether or not they should have more than one child. To pass off making a real decision for themselves on the basis that they must have another child for the sake of the one child they have is to avoid the responsibility for making the decision on their own. If you have another child, do it for yourself because *you* want it, not because you think it is important to your child's emotional health.

TWINS

Though only children do not have a higher percentage of emotional problems than other children, twins statistically do. This is certainly not hard to understand. When you consider how difficult it is for an ordinary person to develop a sense of his own uniqueness and identity and individuality, you can imagine how many more problems a twin will have with this. If the parents blur his individuality even more by dressing him exactly like his twin and emphasizing his being one of a pair rather than a person in his own right, this compounds the damage. Then too twins are bound to feel more of a sense of rivalry and competition with one another than ordinary siblings. Think of how upset some women get when they walk into a party and find that another woman is wearing the exact same dress that they have on. This heightens the comparison between them in other respects and makes them uncomfortable. Well imagine how it must feel to have somebody who looks just like you around all or most of the time. Enough said. Parents of twins must be very careful to highlight their differences and react to them as individuals rather than one of a pair.

The problem with twins starts from the beginning. Mother has a tremendous task. She has two babies to bring up at the same time instead of just one. One is more than enough. She should enlist all the help she can from her husband, mother, and any older siblings. The mother should also use all the short cuts and other aids she can get, such as diaper services, maid service if this is economically feasible, and having neighbors and friends help. With all of this it is difficult to hold two babies at the same time very close—as close as they need to be held. Add to this the pressure and the harassment on the mother and you can understand that there is a fairly good possibility that the twins will not get "good enough" mothering. Breast feeding is possible but difficult. Demand feeding, though also possible, really puts a great strain on the mother.

It is important for the parents to encourage individuality and separateness between the twins. They do not need to be in the same class or engage in the same sports or play the same instruments. They can have separate groups of friends. They certainly should be encouraged as much as possible and the parents should help develop opportunities for them to play with other children. There is always the possibility that they will become too dependent upon one another. Sometimes this even manifests itself by their developing a special system of verbal and non-verbal communication with one another that retards their speech development. This obviously should be discouraged. The key is to recognize that as many problems as we all have establishing our turf and our boundaries, we would be bound to have much greater ones if we had a mirror image (identical twin) or a person of our own age who looked somewhat like us (fraternal twin) around all the time. So the parents must not only help twins "let go" of them but also of each other.

Now that approximately one of three marriages in our country ends in divorce, there are plenty of children around whose parents are divorced.

Perhaps the first issue we should examine is the oft-repeated one: is divorce harmful to children and should a bad marriage be continued for the sake of the children? On this score it seems quite clear to me that, even though children certainly are upset at least for a short time by the disruption of a marriage, in the long run they will almost surely be more upset by being in a home in which there is a bad relationship between the parents. Children are tremendously sensitive to all sorts of emotional fluctuations in the home. Strife between their parents certainly cannot be hidden from them even if the major arguments are kept in private. The tension between two married people who are at odds with one another is so thick it can be cut with a knife. To keep a bad marriage going "for the sake of the children" hardly ever makes any sense. It is much more likely to be used as a rationalization by one or both parents for avoiding their own anxieties about separation from a poor and incompatible choice of mate. It is a very socially acceptable cop-out for people to use who do not have the fortitude to pursue their own wishes and face the challenges the pursuit may bring.

There are so many issues and problems in the handling of children of divorced parents that several excellent books have been written on this subject alone. I will try to hit some of the problems that have not been dealt with so consistently or about which I feel I may have a particularly individual point of view.

I feel quite strongly, for instance, about what parents tell children are the reasons for the divorce, and how they answer questions about the mate they are leaving or have just left. The standard book approach to this has been along the lines of "your father is the most wonderful, kind, loving, courageous man in the world and I respect him tremendously. But somehow, he and I just aren't able to get along together." Now, if mother really feels this, then I think it is fine for her to say it. But if she feels Dad is the most miserable creature that ever walked the face of this earth, I think it is destructive, dishonest, and confusing to a child to hear that euphemistic palaver about him. I do not mean that she should use the children as a sounding board to vilify him and call him every name in the book. But she can be reasonably honest about not liking him if in fact she doesn't. Again the general thesis here, as in almost every section of this book, is that the most important way to be with a child is real and honest. Deception and dishonesty, giving children the correct commercials, the public relations line, is much more damaging than letting them know who you really are and how you really feel—even if you happen to be a miserable, sadistic person. Lies destroy children even more than sadism does.

Another issue that results from divorce is the use of the children to keep the divorced parents from facing their own difficulties in emotional separation. Children are not the only people who have difficulty separating from their mothers. As a matter of fact the failure of the child to effect the process of separation and individuation from the mother results in the displacement of the same problem onto the spouse. When a divorce or separation takes place, to the extent that both parents have not resolved this problem in the course of their own development, there will be a tendency for them to hang on to one another. This hanging on is not out of love. If they have just obtained a divorce, how strong can their love be? Rather it is the result of a failure to be able to cut the cord, a cord that is obviously no longer a viable one. This is where the children often come in. On visiting time for the father, Dad, instead of spending his time with the children, ends up spending all or much of it with Mom to the exclusion of the children. I have seen this situation go on for years and years. One patient of mine continued to see his ex-wife, have meals with her, have intercourse with her and (of course) numerous battles with her for five years after he had left the home. This would occur on so-called visiting days. The wife would be seductive to him, he would respond, and the children were sent off to watch television. Soon Mom and Dad would start arguing. It was a repeat of what had occurred throughout the marriage. It is a good idea for the children's time with the father really to be with him. If possible, the children should be met outside the door and left at the door. Contact between the divorced parents should be kept to a minimum even if the divorce was relatively friendly. Certainly it should be even more minimal if the divorce was a bitter one, as many are.

On the subject of time spent with father, a few words should be said. Many times this becomes a perfunctory duty like visiting a maiden aunt in a nursing home. The same applies to dull, routine, repetitive phone calls from Dad to the children. When Dad spends time with the children, he should really try to figure out what *he* would enjoy doing with them. Going through the motions of taking them to the circus when he happens to hate the circus—as in my case—is not a wise choice of activity. Some things that children love to do also happen to excite some adults. Examples of this might be going to the zoo, hiking through the woods, and going to baseball games. The important point is that the father be there doing something that turns *him* on when he is with the children. Being with him while he is obviously bored and going through the motions and counting the minutes until he can get away merely reinforces the feeling of rejection that the children already have about the father's leaving the home. I say the father's leaving the home not because I necessarily feel this is the way it *should* be, but because 99 percent of the time this is the way it is.

As for the child's feeling rejected and abandoned by the parent, usually the father, who leaves the home, this must be accepted as a fact. No matter how clear it is that the father is leaving the mother and not the child, the child will invariably take it as a personal rejection of himself. It is especially important that the father deal directly with this issue and give the child the opportunity to discuss and air his feelings, including anger and hurt. It is unwise to pretend the child will not or does not feel it. At a time of crisis like that of a divorce in the family it is a good idea for each parent, preferably separately, to have extended conversations and communication of feelings (not the public relations copy) with children. Many parents abdicate their responsibility in this respect and damage the child and their relationship with him.

If a child is under four, there is nothing much to say beyond, "Your mother and I do not love each other and we have decided not to live with each other. But I still love you as much as ever and I will see you twice a week. I want you to tell me how you feel about this and I will try to answer all your questions about it. I feel very badly about it [if you do], and I'm sure you'll be upset in some ways about it." With children over seven I think it makes sense for you to go into your feelings more extensively, so the child really understands your honest reasons for leaving and your plans for the future. With a child over eleven, if you are so inclined and able to, an extensive, communicative discussion in which feelings are expressed by both parent and child is desirable. This dialogue should be continuous, especially over the first six months when the situation may be turbulent emotionally. When the child is between four and eight, how much depth to get into varies with the sophistication of the child and the ability of the parent to communicate.

Needless to say it is unwise to involve the child directly in squabbles about alimony, visitation rights, child support, infidelities and other such issues that belong between the parents and do not involve the child. It might appear that this is a truism but often, before, during, and after divorce, the hostility between the two parents is so great that the child is involved as a pawn to be used to hurt the spouse. Even well-meaning, sophisticated people can find themselves unable to resist this ploy. Being authentic does not mean using your child as a pawn to get at your ex-mate. It is wise to attempt as much as possible to resist it.

Some divorced parents have difficulty with their children about relationships with new people. For instance, patients frequently ask me if it is unwise or harmful for them to sleep with new girl friends or boy friends when the children are staying over with them. Of course, for people with strong religious or moral convictions about sexual activity, this question would not even be raised. With people who have a more "modern" view of sexuality, it seems to me that the children's being aware that the divorced or even separated parent is involved in a sexual relationship with another person is hardly apt to be particularly shocking or destructive to them no matter what their age. If your general approach to sex is to be completely open and permissive about it, then why be hypocritical and pretend that you don't have a sexual relationship with your girl friend or boy friend? Honesty is still the key. Pretense is what destroys. Often being able to sleep with one's lover while having the children stay over makes it easier to be around the children more and does not force an unhappy choice between children and lover that can result in an uncomfortable competition between them and hurt feelings on both sides.

The question sometimes arises in a divorce about which parent the child or children should go to. Unfortunately, custody suits are frequently motivated more by the desire to punish an ex-mate than the desire to have the child. This is really the nth degree of using a child as a pawn and should be avoided at all costs. Make sure that your custody suit is based on a genuine interest in your child's welfare and a conviction of your ability and desire to take care of the child and a sincere belief that you can do it better than your former mate. Men are unfortunately frequently guilty of beginning such suits as a counter to their wives' demands for child support and alimony, which they deem excessive. Then the custody battle is really just a legal maneuver.

Aside from such horrors, assuming both parents genuinely have their children's welfare at heart and are not using this issue to express mutual recriminations, with whom should the children live? I suppose there can be no hard and fast answer to this question. Most of the time courts will award custody to the mother because the father lacks the time, or the skill, or the inclination to take care of the children. This would apply especially to children under ten who require steadier and more continual care. Most fathers in our society have jobs that pretty much preclude the kind of attention younger children require, whereas mothers are usually freer. But with the onset of Women's Liberation, sometimes this is *not* the case. There are also mothers who are, because of inclination, or immaturity, or poor mental or physical health, really unable to take care of their children as well as their husbands. Each situation must be decided on its own merits. Both parents should try to be as objective as possible in determining who will provide the better steady care. The children's wishes in this matter should be a factor, but they should not necessarily be the dominant factor. Letting the children decide whom to go with might be a way for the parents of abdicating an important parental role. You the parent are in a better position to decide who will be the better for your child to be with than the child himself. After all, the child's decision might be based on which parent is the easiest-going, most pleasant, least decisive. Or it might be based on unconscious sexual (Oedipal) attachments. None of these would constitute a valid reason for the choice. You, the parents, should put aside your hostility and take responsibility for deciding which parent would be best for your child to live with, based entirely on that adult's ability and willingness to care for the child.

Another issue that comes up in connection with divorce is whether siblings should be split up. Here too the decision should not be part of a barter. It should be based on how well the siblings do together, how important they are to one another and whether the designated parent has enough time, energy, and skill to deal with more than one child at a time. All things being equal, I suppose in general it is wiser to keep siblings together if they relate well to each other. But as we know, things are often not equal and each situation has to be appraised individually.

If there is no agreement possible between parents on what to do with the children, then a mutual friend trusted by both parents, a doctor, a clergyman or even a psychiatrist or other mental health professional might be able to solve the problem without a prolonged legal battle if both parties agree to accept his decision. This is certainly preferable to a prolonged hassle that is then decided by a judge who may have no training or wisdom in this particular area.

Handling the emotional problems that involve children during the process of divorce and its aftermath is fraught with many pitfalls that can have profound effects on children and on the future of their relationship to both parents. It requires a great deal of skill and psychological sophistication that many parents may not possess. It might be wise to consider seeking the help of a trusted friend or a professional in handling questions difficult for you to answer alone.

ADOPTING CHILDREN

The most important contributions that the newer discoveries in the field of child development can make to parents who are thinking about adopting a child has to do with the age of adoption. From what we have seen up to this point, it is clear that the first year and even the first months or weeks are very crucial periods in the development of a child. With this in mind I very strongly recommend that adoption should take place at the earliest possible moment—within the first week of life if possible. I can recall the parents of a twenty-year-old girl who was adopted at the age of five months. By all objective standards they were loving, interested, understanding, responsible parents. Yet their daughter had all sorts of disturbing emotional problems. The mother was beset by guilt. What had she done to produce such a disturbed, unhappy young woman as a daughter? I remember I had to reassure her repeatedly that there was no evidence that either she or her husband had been destructive to the girl. Almost from the very beginning of their contact with her, she had exhibited difficulties—feeding problems, colic,

148 fears, school problems, difficulties with her peers. At each succeeding age level the problems became more and more pronounced. The parents did their best to cope with these problems but they were fighting a losing battle.

Now I do not want to sound too much like an alarmist. I am sure that some of you can give me examples of later or even late adoptions that have worked out quite well. But lying in a crib in an institution or being cared for by a neglectful mother during the first months or year of life can have very serious effects on the emotional development of a child that may be difficult to reverse. Of course, some children seem to have such an extraordinary genetic and constitutional endowment that they appear able to survive almost any degree of trauma. I often am amazed at how much health and strength my patients exhibit in the face of the experiences they have endured. But still—certainly if there is a choice—I would choose to adopt a baby at age five days rather than five months. As far as adoption of older children goes, I would be very much concerned about their past experiences and especially the quality of the mothering they have received. An adopted child can be a boon, but he can also be a nightmare that can make the life of the new parent extremely difficult.

As far as the usual questions about whether to tell a child he is adopted and how and when to tell him about it, I think most people in the field are in general agreement. The child should certainly know he is adopted. For one thing he might find out at some time in a way that would shock or embarrass or hurt him. For another this book has been stressing all along that parents should be real and authentic. To keep a secret from a child would hamper their spontaneity with that child. Besides that, if the child found out later that they had been lying to him all along (and this would be most probable) the discovery would certainly erode his confidence and trust in them. Parents should always be completely honest in discussing the adoption if and when it ever comes up. A child under three would probably not ask questions that referred to it. But as a three and four year old finds out about the birth process, he might ask, "Did I come out of your stomach?"

At this point you could answer truthfully, "No you did not. Another woman carried you and gave birth to you. But she could not take care of you, so I took you." Then as the child grew older, explanations could become more detailed. The knowledge of his adoption should evolve gradually as with sexual knowledge. He should not be *sat down* to have the whole thing explained at one particular moment.

THE HANDICAPPED CHILD

A handicapped child can be quite a problem for a family. Among the more common handicaps are retardation, childhood schizophrenia, crossed eyes, blindness, deafness, cerebral palsy, anatomical defects from hereditary causes, or birth defects. I shall not go into the handling of the defects themselves; this is better left to pediatricians or specialists in these illnesses.

The problems that arise from these handicaps that a psychoanalyst can shed some light on are those that arise in the parents, notably the mothers of these children, or in their siblings. I have never with one exception had a patient with a handicap in twenty-five years of practice. But I have had many many of their siblings. This fact in itself bears scrutiny.

First let us deal with the problems of mothers of handicapped babies or children. A major difficulty for these mothers is in handling what they experience as a serious narcissistic wound in having such a child. The child is seen unconsciously as an extension of their own body. If a mother has problems (and many of us do) about her own body image, then it is as if the handicapped child represents a destruction of part of this image. The unconscious result of this is a feeling of rage both against fate and against the child. Of course, feeling this rage is totally unacceptable to the conscious part of the mind and often produces guilt. In many cases the rage is repressed through the overt expression of overconcern and overprotectiveness. What often can happen that is really bad for the handicapped child—almost as bad as his handicap—is that the mother will go out of her way to favor him, protect him and make him into a psychological invalid on top of his being handicapped. Of course, the best attitude would be one of honest acceptance of his handicap, giving him any actual help that the handicap requires and then, beyond this, treating him as a normal person. The parents' problems so frequently interfere with this happening that I am tempted to advise every parent of a handicapped child to seek some counseling. Organizations that deal with handicaps, such as United Cerebral Palsy, National Association for Retarded Children, Muscular Dystrophy Association, and others, usually have such counseling available to parents. Pediatricians, psychologists, and psychiatrists can also be extremely helpful with short-term counseling concerning this issue.

The mother's giving an excess of time and attention to the handicapped child, especially if it is a compulsive reaction to guilt about rage over a narcissistic wound, is likely to have a major effect on the siblings of the child. And, as I said before, they are the ones who have constituted a large percentage of my practice. These siblings are really in a double bind. They are tremendously deprived of "good enough mothering" by their handicapped siblings, but at the same time pick up the mother's guilt about *her* hostility toward the child and so are left with a rage at being deprived, guilt about feeling the rage and no place to turn the rage except upon themselves. Therefore the classic picture they present later in life is a tendency to be depressed, masochistic and self-destructive. They also frequently feel sorry for themselves over some alleged misfortune. They thus tend to identify with their sibling and become "handicapped" adults, feeling they deserve special sympathy and special treatment like their sibling received in their childhood.

It suffices from just this much to see clearly that a very pathological family interaction can grow around a handicapped child. The effects can be very long term. Parents of such children should definitely seek counseling to reduce the impact of the problem on the child as well as the rest of the family.

If you are a dedicated male chauvinist, don't bother to read this section. Insist on your point of view and try to raise your children according to your own dictates if you and your wife are in agreement! If, on the other hand, you believe in some of the ideas and ideals of Women's Liberation, you as a parent can do a great deal to help your children to grow up with these attitudes rather than having to adjust to them as something new as, I am sure, you have. As a parent who is to whatever degree a feminist, you must realize that there are certain things you can do directly with your children, and that you will have to work hard to counter some of the strong influences they are bound to be subjected to by what is essentially a very strongly biased male chauvinist culture.

One of the most important things you can do is try to treat the girls in the same manner as you treat the boys if you happen to have children of both sexes. That means having the boys just as involved in buying groceries, cooking, washing dishes, setting the table, as the girls are. Conversely it means having the girls as involved in "traditional male" duties such as taking out the garbage, mowing the lawn, painting, shoveling snow, doing mechanical repair work around the house, as the boys are. It also means that you do not buy the girls all the dolls and the boys the erector sets—that you try to listen in order to get them what each really wants, but beyond that, that you try to compensate for cultural influences a bit by pushing the erector sets on the girls and the dolls on the boys. It means you play ball as much with the girls as with the boys. It means later on that you handle the issue of sexual freedom equally. It also means that when your little girl says she wants to be a nurse when she grows up, you openly question why she wouldn't perhaps prefer to be a doctor.

I have seen several female patients with tremendous problems that arose at least in part from their having had brothers who were strongly and obviously favored over them, clearly on the basis of sex. These women, many of whom were extraordinarily intelligent and capable, developed a exaggeratedly defective image of themselves, did poorly in school despite superior endowment, ended up marrying men who dominated and disparaged them and only began to get in touch with their real selves after many years of psychoanalysis. Many, many women in our culture view themselves emotionally (whatever they may *think* intellectually) as inferior to men intellectually and physically, as unable to be effective in the performance of independent activity. Our culture is constantly reinforcing these ideas. As parents you will have to combat openly anti-female remarks you hear from others, see on television, so your little girl will see that there is point of view different from what she is generally exposed to outside her home.

Of course, the most effective way to impart these ideas is by your own example. Again it is one thing to talk, but another to act. Actions very definitely speak louder than words. Do you as the father share in the care of the house and children? Does your wife drive the car as much as you? Does she handle the finances? Does she pursue a separate career as well as her household duties? Some of you correctly will say it is too much to ask of yourself to make the total leap from male chauvinism to feminism in a period of ten years. You can say perhaps correctly that it will take generations to bring about all of these changes. You do have a point there, but you can also use that to cop out on making the changes you profess to desire so strongly. One thing that you, the mother, can do if you are really sincere, is to get involved in a women's consciousness-raising group.

You, the reader, might wonder why I am going out of my way to include so much feminist material in a book mainly concerned with raising children. The reason for this is not so that I can slip a little propaganda in on a captive audience. Rather, I believe that this issue is without a doubt the most profound one in our era. I think that male-female relationships have been clearly set in a mold that involves masculine power and domination and passive aggressive retaliations on the part of the female. An example, indeed a classic barometer of this gross perversion of the manner in which people can relate to one another is in the sexual area, when the male pursues and often uses the female as an object, and the female retaliates by withholding. But this pattern pervades all of the relationship between them, not only the sexual one. This kind of sadomasochism basically precludes closeness and real love between them and sets up a constant battle and a great deal of unpleasantness. It is a situation that has been pervasive in our culture and has undoubtedly caused tremendous inner hostility that has then been expressed in a group manner through war and other destructive means. That is why I feel that an important part of bringing up a child, whether male or female, today, is to try to stem the tide of this horror, to help to give your children the possibility of a different kind of relationship to the opposite sex and a different kind of feeling about themselves as people.

——————————ADOLESCENCE: SPECIAL PROBLEMS INCLUDING SEX, TOBACCO, MARIJUANA, ALCOHOL AND DRUGS

Several excellent books have been written specifically about the relationship between adolescents and their parents. Since the focus of this book is not specifically on adolescence, I will deal merely with some specific problems that occur only or mainly in adolescence. Those years, roughly between twelve and eighteen, are years of great flux in every possible way—in terms of physical growth, sexual, intellectual, and social development, and character definition and formation. Things are happening so quickly and changing in so many directions at once that there is an unstable quality that characterizes the period. In retrospect I cannot see how I ever managed to get through my adolescence and certainly would not want to go through it again. I think most of us feel that way about it. Those years are truly an age of anxiety. So many choices about new directions need to be made. And, of course, adolescence should be an important period for breaking emotional ties with parents, for discarding their values and forming values of our own, for beginning to see ourselves as separate adults rather than satellites of our parents. It can be an especially difficult time for both parents and children.

Adolescence is also the period characterized by inconsistency and opposites. Impulses are attempting to break through into the core of the personality. At times they gush like a flood and appear to come close to overwhelming the more stable, structured part of the personality. Then, at other times, these same impulses are very strongly pushed back and defended against. That is why we can see contrasts in the same person, sometimes within the same week, of hedonism and asceticism, pleasure-seeking and pleasure-denying. Or an adolescent may be uninhibited in one area and totally repressed in another; he may indulge in excesses in sex or alcohol or drugs while he is a vegetarian who pays strict attention to his diet! He may become very much involved in a spartan religious denomination and shortly thereafter indulge in what seems to be a totally disorganized, unstructured way of life. There are often strong and strange contrasts between enormous idealism, altruism, self-sacrifice, and care about the disadvantaged, side by side with what seems to be the most egocentric, selfish, rude, and thoughtless behavior causing great hurt to others. The only consistency, then, is the inconsistency, and the only thing that is predictable is the unpredictability. This means a strong, firm parental structure is essential to provide a matrix, a center, from which the adolescent can separate himself.

This will really be a time when all of the correct steps —and the incorrect ones—you have taken in rearing your child will come home to roost. If you have held them very close during their first years, when they needed it, you will have established a basic climate of trust. Thus even when your adolescent needs to rebel against you and disagree with you, break away from your value system in the process of establishing his own identity, autonomy, and individuality, it will still be within a framework of a general feeling of love and respect for you, the parents. On the other hand, if he has harbored hostility and resentment because you were not sufficiently responsive to his needs during the early years, then the normal rebellion will be escalated by some old hatreds. The teen-ager's reactions will then appear to be totally outrageous and inappropriate to what the current stimulus is. The structure during the earlier years of the teen-ager's life that contained and repressed these impulses is suddenly loosened. A great many impulses from the past as well as current and physiologically newer sexual impulses begin to break through. Sexual impulses toward parents also have a strong impetus during this period and may be defended against by hostility toward or sudden avoidance of contact with the parent of the opposite sex. It is not uncommon for an adolescent daughter who ostensibly had a good relationship with her father to cut him off and literally not speak to him for months (even years!) during this period.

Of course, the same applies—perhaps even more—to how you have handled the "let them go" part of childrearing. Hopefully you will have let them engage in a gradual and appropriate amount of separation from you from the early years on. You will have allowed them as much autonomy as they could handle. And you would have consistently been authentic and real in dealing with them, so they had a consistently clear view of you as a person in your own right with your own ideas and needs different and separate from theirs. If this has been the case, much of the task of separation will already have been accomplished before the adolescent period. Adolescence will merely be a smooth continuation of that development. There will still be other problems for the adolescent, such as handling his sexual and other impulses, professional, social, and intellectual maturation, and many others. But at least the problem of separation will have been accomplished to a large extent.

What will the results be if you have not "let them go"?

Well, one result might be that the child never goes through adolescence at all. He passes through the years from twelve to eighteen and maybe even through twenty, thirty, fifty, and seventy, and remains emotionally an unseparated child. He has no opinions or goals of his own; he follows your way or his wife's or his boss's or anyone else's who proclaims himself a leader. He has no sense of self, strikes other people as being immature and of no substance. I have seen many adults like this from ages twenty to seventy-five. They are unmistakable to a psychiatrist, but they do not appear bizarre or strange to most people. Their discomfort is mostly inside, subjective. As these children pass through adolescence *without going through adolescence,* they remain compliant children who work hard, do well in school, do not mix much with their peers and have relatively little overt interest in sex. They may be referred to by their peers as "Mama's boys" or "Goody-Two-Shoes" or "Professional virgins." If your child goes through adolescence without ever giving you any trouble at all or without being interested in sex, don't count these too soon as blessings. In one way or another, you have either kept the child too close too long or have not let him go. Instead of congratulating yourself, it is better to recognize that your holding on might possibly result in a perpetual child who cannot really grow up. It may or may not be too late to try to push him into more freedom, more physical and emotional separations from you and more social and sexual activity. Sometimes pushing a child at this point just makes the situation more painful. However, diagnosing the problem and attempting to cope with it at age twelve is a lot better than waiting until age eighteen. An adolescent of eighteen can say with considerable justification, "You always taught me to be a good, hard-working, asexual kid who ought to listen to you and worship your every word, who should never be aggressive and never fight back, stay home and do my homework. Now, all of a sudden, you want me to transform myself into some free, assertive, sexual, socially adept person! What do you think I am?" If whatever pressure you put on your adolescent only makes him feel more anxious and even more painfully aware of his deficiencies and his differences from his peers, then it might be wise to consider professional help. There is a good chance it will be required anyway, later on, and the earlier it is instituted the better.

But sometimes not "letting go" all along the way at the appropriate times can have a different result. If there has been some "letting go" but not enough or an inconsistency in the "letting go," then this may result in a tremendous internal upheaval in the child and a concomitant storm in the parent-child relationships. In this instance the child is caught between a push to separate and a fear of doing it. Attempts to separate, rather than representing a smooth advance on a continuum, may occur in fits and starts and explosions. The adolescent may indulge in all sorts of rebellious behavior, such as truancy, drinking, anti-social behavior, taking drugs, and so on, in an attempt to burst out. Then, sheepishly, he or she may retreat to a completely immature, childish dependency upon the parents. Adolescents like this usually have emotional problems for which professional help is a good idea. Sometimes they are treated individually or in groups with their peers. Lately, there has been a decided swing in the direction of family therapy: the whole family is treated as a unit. This represents an acknowledgment that the problem involves the entire family and must be treated as such. Adolescence is a time when you will be very grateful that you have established a firm structure and a strong relationship of authority between yourself and your child. Or conversely you will be extremely regretful that you have not. The chances of your maintaining any kind of order or discipline now will be very poor unless you have already established it beforehand when you had more power and your child had more self-control. You must expect a certain amount of rebellion, but there are acceptable and unacceptable ways of expressing it, and you must be the judge of which is which.

Let us discuss some of the more common troubles that arise at this period. One is the use of tobacco. As the Surgeon General reminds us on every package of cigarettes, smoking can be injurious to your health. Almost everyone in the field of medicine with the exception of the doctors and scientists in the pay of the tobacco industry seems to agree that the heavier the amount of smoking the greater the risk of cancer and cardiovascular and pulmonary diseases. This is so unequivocal that whether you personally happen to be a cigarette smoker or not, it seems to me that while you have the power to control, you should absolutely forbid the use of tobacco, at least as far as cigarettes. Even if you yourself are a smoker and for whatever reason have not been able to stop, you should know that what you are doing is very self-destructive, and you should not want to inflict this habit on your children. Some people work on the theory that if you allow children to smoke at will, they will not express their rebellion in this particular way. This view may have some merit, but my own feeling is that outright prohibition probably works better. Adolescents are often interested in good health, naturalness and anti-pollution measures. Many of them will take stands against smoking as strong as your own, so your child will hardly be ostracized or feel "out" among his group of peers if he does not smoke. You can prohibit his smoking in the house. You cannot exert absolute control over him when he is away from you, but you have to hope that your personal explanations to him of the dangers of smoking plus the general educational program against smoking will pay off. Of course, if you yourself or your mate is a heavy smoker, you will be double binding your child again. Perhaps this will help you to make an attempt to give it up so you can be a good model for your child. But if not, you have to hope the influences you and the culture exert against smoking will in this respect outweigh your child's tendency to model himself after you.

One of the most frequent problems that parents must deal with in adolescents is the smoking of marijuana and the use of other drugs. It seems to me from the accumulation of evidence that marijuana is a relatively safe, harmless drug pharmacologically—much safer than alcohol. I am very much in favor of legalizing its use for people over twenty-one. But just as strongly as I favor its legalization for adults, so I oppose its use by adolescents and children. In the schools, children under ten are beginning to use it. Certainly among eleven or twelve years olds its use is rampant and seems to increase through college age. Even though the pharmacological effects of marijuana may be minimal (though some studies have indicated that heavy use does cause minimal brain damage), the psychological effect of its use is tremendously destructive. I have seen many adolescents as well as young adults who have used marijuana so heavily and consistently over a period of years that they have essentially withdrawn from any meaningful contact with people and any attempt to fulfill their creative potential. Marijuana is so easily available and can give such a pleasant, euphoric sensation that people use it to avoid any challenges that arise in their scholastic, intellectual and even social-sexual life. Two young people, instead of working out a problem in their relationship, will smoke and avoid it. I know many relatively young parents who smoke marijuana occasionally themselves and are very permissive about the use of it by their adolescent children. I am strongly against this point of view. I think that children and adolescents do not have enough emotional maturity or inner controls to regulate their use of marijuana. Not only can excessive and improper use of the drug in childhood be destructive in itself, but it very often can lead to the use of other drugs —so-called soft drugs, and then on occasion even hard drugs. People must reckon with the fact that hard drug use is no longer limited to lower-class minority groups. Anyone who is a parent to an adolescent must accept the fact that there is a clear and present danger that their child may take such drugs. Of course, the horrors and the self-destruction that these drugs wreak is now commonly known. One of my neighbors had a nineteen-year-old daughter die from an overdose of heroin recently. The chances are good that one of the adolescents in your neighborhood may be on heroin. If you draw the line very firmly at the use of marijuana, the chances are good that you can effectively stop the use of other drugs such as mescaline, LSD, cocaine and heroin. My feeling is that you should be very alert to the possibility of the use of marijuana by your adolescent child. You are not being paranoid to suspect that he or she will use it. Look out for telltale signs, such as the smell of the drug, cigarette papers, a lackadaisical, uninvolved attitude. If you discover that the teen-ager is in a group of peers who are marijuana users, I feel that very very strong measures are indicated to discourage his association with them. Being one of a herd is a tremendously strong motivation in adolescents. They wear the same kind of clothes as their peer group, use the same language, and begin to break away from the parental orbit by strengthening their connections with peer groups. This is a normal process. To expect your child to belong to a group of peers whose activity involves to a major or even minor degree smoking marijuana and *not* smoke is the height of foolishness. You must do whatever you can and at as early an age as you can to stop these associations. This can include not allowing any of the group in your house, not allowing calls from them, prohibiting as much as you can association with them during the day (though this may be impossible at school) and "grounding" your child—not allowing him out of the house evenings or weekends. These may appear to be extremely strong measures to keep your son or daughter from using a little "pot." But if you have seen, as I have, children whose lives have been destroyed by it, whose academic, professional and social-sexual life has been ruined, then you might not feel that these kinds of measures were too drastic. Of course, along with this it is very important to have a reassuring dialogue with your child explaining in depth your point of view and trying to make it clear that you are not just being arbitrary and rigid but have his best interest in mind.

Alcohol use among adolescents is a new problem that is apparently on the rise. I was shocked to read a report about ten- and eleven-year-old alcoholics. This might seem a bit far-fetched (I know I still find it hard to believe), but I certainly can believe that many children from eleven on up are raiding their parents' alcohol supply in their absence and getting high on it. Apparently as there is a slight decrease in the use of marijuana and soft and hard drugs, there has been a substantial increase in the use of alcohol. Now I think alcohol is a boon to mankind, can help one relax, get one over sexual anxiety, increase one's enjoyment of a party. "Malt does more than Milton can/To justify God's ways toward man." So I am very, very far from being a teetotaler or a prohibitionist. But again, as with marijuana, I do not feel that most children or adolescents have the maturity or self-discipline to use this drug wisely. And unlike marijuana which is not addicting, alcohol of course can be extremely addicting. Even if you find it hard to believe that you may have an eleven-year-old alcoholic, I am sure you will not find it difficult to believe you can have a nineteen-year-old alcoholic. Aside from its addictive potential, alcohol by adolescents can be used to escape from dealing with problems that challenge them just as they can use marijuana and other drugs. It is too tempting for an adolescent, who has so many difficult problems to face, to have access to any substance that can help him avoid these issues.

Whether you think of sex as a big adolescent problem depends upon your own particular point of view about the desirability or undesirability of sexual activities among adolescents. Whatever your views may be about this, however, I am sure there will be no disagreement that avoiding unwanted pregnancies and venereal disease is desirable. For this reason either you or someone you trust to do the job well should inform your children about these matters at least by the time they enter puberty. Knowledge, as I have said before, is not the same as license. How you handle what you tell them about sex will vary a great deal. Some of you will feel that any sexual activity is permissible as soon as there is a desire for it. Others for religious or other reasons will feel that no sexual activity before marriage is permissible. Whatever your particular beliefs, try to communicate them, along with your reasons, to your children. Set very clear rules and limits about curfews and sexual and dating behavior. Many, many parents avoid the whole issue of talking about sex with their children because of their own discomfort and embarrassment about it. Whatever your personal views or beliefs may be about sex in adolescence, you are really abdicating an important responsibility if you do not attempt to talk to your children about it at length. You may be avoiding a great deal of strife and misunderstanding and mutual recrimination if you do communicate with your children about it. Whatever it is you believe, you have the right, authority, and obligation to have imposed it upon your child when younger.

Another important problem is that of maintaining discipline and respect with adolescents while still encouraging the expression of negative feelings, of which there may be an abundance. Here it is important to be clear on the distinction between expressing what *you* feel toward another person and your putting down or disparaging or showing a lack of respect for that person. There is a subtle but very clear distinction between saying "I hate you" and saying, "you are a stupid, idiotic son of a bitch." The former is acceptable because it expresses a feeling clearly and directly. The latter is not, because it attempts to vilify another person. Of course, if you expect your adolescent to follow this excellent rule of acceptable communication versus unacceptable personal attack, then you would be well advised to apply the same rules to yourself in your dealing with him. But it is tremendously important that you insist on maintaining a level of respect. If you, like Rodney Dangerfield, "don't get no respect" from your adolescent, you are both apt to be in a good deal of trouble.

Aside from these more serious problems, how does a parent handle his feeling about the length of a teen-ager's hair, the type of clothes he chooses to wear, the music he likes to hear? All of these are in fact attempts to be different from parents and to separate from them. In that sense they are harmless and non-destructive ways of expressing individuality. But suppose you absolutely can't stand acid-rock, as I admit freely that I can't? Well, what I do is simply make it clear that there will be none of that played in any part of the house that is within my hearing when I am home. On the other hand, my teen-agers are free to play it at will within the confines of their rooms or when I am out of the house. With difficulty I try to contain myself in putting down this music to them, though I must admit to occasional slips! In compensation I allow them equally to put down the music I like—Benny Goodman, Glenn Miller, and others from "the medieval era" as my son calls it.

Hair length and choice of dress are a bit more difficult to handle since they cannot be banished so easily without banishing the teen-ager along with them. If you really have it clearly etched in your mind that this expression of individuality and difference from you is a necessary step in their development, which it is, then perhaps it may make you somewhat more tolerant and capable of being oblivious. Taking strong and punitive stands against these harmless forms of self-expression or constantly nagging at or disparaging adolescents because of them is likely to push them into much more destructive ways of expressing their separateness from you. You may say at this point, "What kind of separateness or uniqueness is that? Every kid on the block looks alike!" But remember, the separateness is *from you*. It is important that they have allies in their siblings or peers in this enormous and difficult struggle to become independent of you.

Another important issue for an adolescent is that there should be a change in his status reflected in the way he is treated in the home. In primitive tribes there are puberty rites that mark this time. In the Jewish religion there is the bar mitzvah or bas mitzvah. In Christianity there is the confirmation ceremony. When a child moves into puberty or adolescence, an acknowledgment by the parents is required, formal or otherwise. This means that the teen-ager should now be treated as a young adult rather than a child. He should have more privileges, privacy, decision-making powers, and general autonomy. Failure to recognize this change in his status may bring about deserved hostility. As part of "letting go," parents should try to maintain a certain distance from an adolescent. An adolescent should not be required to reveal everything. There ought to be areas of his private and personal life that are no longer part of the parents' domain. He needs his own turf. His mail should not be opened. His drawers should not be opened and examined. His diary should not be read. All such parental behavior helps the adolescent to negotiate the difficult process of separation—the separation that was gone through originally on another level in the second and third years of life.

With the sudden and rapid increase in sexual feelings at this period, there is also a tremendous increase in the focus on narcissism and body-image concerns. Adolescents become extremely sensitive about their appearance. They are terribly concerned about being too fat, too thin, too short, too tall or having any blemish or any feature that is different or unusual. They can become very upset about a mole or protruding ears or heavy ankles. Perhaps this is a function in part of our society's great emphasis on physical attractiveness as a prerequisite to sexual satisfaction. Later on, of course, we realize that this equation is not valid. Beauty does not necessarily promise sexual happiness. But an adolescent often feels that he will never be able to obtain a sexual partner because he is not classically handsome or beautiful. Acne has certainly been the bane of many adolescents' existence. Parents must be very careful about teasing their children about physical defects, especially at this age. Adolescents need positive responses from their parents during these years to help heal wounds to their narcissism. *Authentic sexual* responses from parents to children of the opposite sex telling them how beautiful or cute or handsome they are can be very great boons to those teen-agers who see themselves as ugly. This cannot, of course, be insincere. If your teen-ager really is going through a bad stage in terms of appearance, don't fake praise you don't feel. However their negative feelings about themselves are usually quite exaggerated. This narcissism applies to things other than the body. Parents should make strong attempts not to be destructive about their adolescents' ideas, thinking, judgment, or tastes. This certainly does not mean the parent should falsely agree with statements that appear incorrect. But it is one thing to disagree and quite another to be destructive. There is a difference between saying, "Now that is just plain stupid; you must really be a moron," and saying, "I really don't see it your way. I think such and such."

With all this good advice, there will nevertheless be times when there just appears to be no way to find a mutually agreeable solution to a conflict between an adolescent and his parents. He may insist on staying out till midnight (as all the other boys do) and you may just as strongly insist that that is too late at his age. Now what? Well, after you have tried to stretch your own flexibility as far as it can go, and with all due respect for his need for autonomy, there is *no way* you are going to let him stay out till midnight. At this point, you have the right, and the duty as well, to use everything in your power to enforce your rule. By late adolescence, sometimes the only power you have is economic. So you must make it clear that if he violates curfew (or breaks whatever other rule you are in disagreement about), then you will be forced to dock his allowance or withhold financial support for his summer camp or his skis or whatever else you contribute. This is your basic power and you must use it to enforce your position. When your adolescent becomes self-supporting, you no longer have or should have control over him. Making the rules and the specific punishment for infractions clear and firm can go a long way toward avoiding misunderstandings that may escalate into serious disruptions. Inconsistency in applying your own rules leads to a great many avoidable problems.

Some of the other issues that are important in adolescence have been dealt with in other sections of the book. Needless to say in this period a parent has to walk a very tight line between being so restrictive and rigid that he will impede his child's development as an individual and being so permissive that he will allow an adolescent whose judgment is often not the best to embark on some really self-destructive course that may be irreversible. This is no easy matter, and it will require your best in understanding, patience, tact, and good judgment.

SPECIAL PROBLEMS REQUIRING———————
PROFESSIONAL HELP

Without going into any detail, I would like to mention some problems that should signal a parent that professional consultation is indicated. These are tip-of-the iceberg symptoms as they nearly always indicate some deeper and more widespread continued difficulty. To my mind more than the relief of the particular symptom is required, even if symptom relief can be effected in a behavioral way. These symptoms indicate that a more comprehensive investigation is in order. One such symptom is bed-wetting that persists in a consistent way—not just on rare occasions—past age four or five. This symptom, assuming physical reasons have been eliminated as causative, usually indicates some hostility in a child toward a parent he views as inordinately or unfairly authoritarian. Mechanical or pharmacological ways of eliminating the symptom are only band-aids, since they do not attack the root problem. Another such symptom is stuttering. This too in my mind requires more than a speech therapist, as skilled as many of them may be. It also is a signal of a profound disturbance in the parent-child relationship. Another such symptom is a major identification with the opposite sex—effeminate behavior in a boy or masculine behavior in a girl. This is a very complicated subject and I have been a strong advocate of *not* seeing homosexuality as some dreaded disease. However such behavior in a child does bear investigation.

Obviously serious disabilities in learning how to read should also be investigated. If psychological tests show that there is no retardation, this too can be a manifestation of emotional difficulty. Imaginary playmates bear looking into. As I have said above, persistent phobias—fear of the dark, animals, thunder and lightning—should herald professional consultation. Hyperactivity is often a symptom of some organic brain dysfunction, but it can also be caused by psychological problems. Sleep disturbances and severe eating problems also bear investigation, as well as chronic diarrhea or constipation. Of course serious and persistent behavior disorders at home or at school may also be symptoms of some difficulty in the family; these would include stealing, fighting with other children, truancy, vandalism, fire-setting. Tics are very frequently emotionally caused and treatable. Generalized anxiety, night terrors and frequent nightmares also indicate some difficulty. Obsessions—thoughts that are repeated over and over—and compulsions—behavior that must be carried out repeatedly—are also important symptoms. Excessive day-dreaming or wandering of attention should also not be overlooked. Obviously, later in childhood, the use of alcohol, marijuana, and drugs requires professional consultation.

The above are only a few frequent symptoms that occur in children. Obviously there may be others. It seems to me that it is better to have a few unnecessary consultations than to have one too few. You can start out by asking your general practitioner or pediatrician, if you think he is psychologically sophisticated. However, some of them are not. In that case, you must look around to find someone who is competent in this particular field. That may not be so easy, but your local medical or psychological society may help you find a specialist in children's emotional problems.

I recognize, however, that finding the right kind of professional help can often be a problem for someone whose child requires treatment. Unfortunately there are not as many well-trained professionals in child psychiatry or child psychology as there ought to be. And many people who are reasonably well trained in handling adults are quite inadequate when it comes to diagnosing or treating children. If you live in a small town or even in a small city, there may not be anyone in the immediate vicinity who has adequate training or background. In such places, the best person to inquire of is someone who is in the general field. For instance, if there is a psychiatrist in town who does not have training with children's problems, he may know of another professional nearby who does. If there is a Child Guidance Clinic in town or a Community Mental

Health Clinic that accepts children, this is usually a good bet. The competence of the specific person who handles your problem will, of course, vary. Degrees, previous training and experience are somewhat important. But do not fail to honor your own impression of the therapist. If he or she appears confident and handles situations in a calm, intelligent, and professional manner, you can feel good about trusting him. If you get a negative impression, ask to be transferred to someone else if it is a clinic. If it is a private office, simply don't return, and seek someone else.

In a large city, the chances of finding a well-trained adequate professional are much better and, in fact, you may very well have a choice of many. In general the best judges of a person's competence are his colleagues, in his specific field. The best way to make a choice is to ask a friend who is in the general field or ask among your friends if any of them knows a professional who could make a recommendation for a referral.

Your general practitioner, pediatrician or clergyman might help, though often they are not as well informed about the specific competence of a child therapist as someone who is in that specific field. In big cities there are usually family care agencies that generally have rather high standards of professionalism. Going to one of these would be safer than picking a private practitioner, unless you have a specific recommendation from one of his colleagues. In some communities school guidance counselors or principals may be able to make recommendations. But again, it would be good to check these recommendations with someone specifically in the professional field of helping children with their emotional problems.

SUMMARY

I have attempted to describe some insights into child-rearing based on the newer research in psychoanalytic theory, especially in the area of child development. The results of this research emphasize the importance of a very close, loving, adoring relationship with a child, especially during the first two years of life, followed by a gradual letting go of the child and the encouragement of independence and individuality. One of the main ways a parent can encourage his child's emotional separation from himself is to be real and express his own individuality rather than play some stereotyped role as an "ideal parent." The application of these ideas has been examined in various aspects of child-rearing. The two central ideas that run through this book are to "hold them very very close; then let them go" and as a parent to "be yourself—not what you think you ought to be." Be an authentic person and you will be a better parent.

INDEX

G

H

I

J

K

L